KAUTILYANOMICS FOR MODERN TIMES

KAUTILYANOMICS FOR MODERN TIMES

Sriram Balasubramanian

BLOOMSBURY
NEW DELHI • LONDON • OXFORD • NEW YORK • SYDNEY

BLOOMSBURY INDIA
Bloomsbury Publishing India Pvt. Ltd
Second Floor, LSC Building No. 4, DDA Complex, Pocket C – 6 & 7,
Vasant Kunj, New Delhi 110070

BLOOMSBURY, BLOOMSBURY INDIA and the Diana logo
are trademarks of Bloomsbury Publishing Plc

First published in India 2022
This edition published 2022

ISBN: PB: 978-93-54350-36-8; e-Book: 978-93-54350-52-8
4 6 8 10 9 7 5 3

Typeset in Fournier MT Std by Manipal Technologies Limited
Printed and bound in India Gopsons Papers Pvt. Ltd., Noida.

To my late grandmother, Jambakam Ramamurthy, who made me who I am today, and for that I will be eternally grateful.

I am thankful to my wife, Lakshmi, our son, Skanda Sriram, and my parents, Sharadha Balasubramanian and R. Balasubramanian.

॥श्रीगुरुभ्यो नमः ॥
हर हर शङ्कर जय जय शङ्कर!

अयं बन्धुरयंनेति गणना लघुचेतसाम्
उदारचरितानां तु वसुधैव कुटुम्बकम ॥

The distinction, 'this person is mine, and this one is not', is made only by the narrow-minded (the ignorant who are in duality). For those of noble conduct (those who know the Supreme Truth), the whole world is one family (one unit).

—Mantra VI-72, *Maha Upanishad*

प्रजासुखे सुखं राज्ञः प्रजानां च हिते हितम् ।
नात्मप्रियं हितं राज्ञः प्रजानां तु प्रियं हितम् (01.19.34)

A king's happiness lies in the happiness of his subjects, and his welfare in the welfare of his subjects; a king's welfare consists not in what pleases him but in what pleases his subjects.

—*The Kautilya Arthashastra*, Kangle 1965

CONTENTS

MAPS

FIGURES

TABLES

FOREWORD

This book by Sriram Balasubramanian has a reference to the Insolvency and Bankruptcy Code (IBC), enacted in May 2016, and the Insolvency and Bankruptcy Board of India (IBBI), formally established on 1 October 2016. On 1 October 2021, five years after IBBI was established, I was invited to deliver the board's Fifth Annual Day Lecture. In search of an apt aphorism, I picked on लालयेत् पञ्च वर्षाणि दश वर्षाणि ताडयेत्। प्राप्ते तु षोडशे वर्षे पुत्रं मित्रवदाचरेत्॥ 'Nurture a son for the first five years, chastise him for the subsequent 10 years. When he attains the age of 16 years, treat him like a friend.'

Most people have heard this. It belongs to the class of what is called, in Samskritam, subhashitam, meaning 'good saying'. It is also attributed to 'Chanakya Niti'. In economics, if there is a clever saying that is apocryphal and one doesn't know who it should be attributed to, one often opts for John Maynard Keynes. In literature, if there is a clever saying and one doesn't know who it should be attributed to, one often opts for Oscar Wilde. In a similar vein, for anything connected with governance in old Indian texts, the temptation is to attribute it to Kautilya.

Kautilya is the accepted spelling now, though if one follows the gotra, Kautalya is more accurate. Acharya

Hemachandra belonged to the eleventh and twelfth centuries. He wrote extensively, though many of his works have been lost now. He was also a lexicographer and composed a lexicon known as *Abhidhan-Chintamani*. In that, various names are given for the same individual—Vatsyayana, Mallanaga, Kautilya, Dramila, Chanaka's son (Chanakya), Pakshilasvami, Vishnugupta and Angula. Yes, indeed, other lexicons (*Vaijayanti*, *Trikandasesa* and *Namamalika* are other examples) have equated Vatsyayana, author of the *Kamasutra*, with Kautilya, author of the *Arthashastra*.

Today, if we know about Kautilya as the author of the *Arthashastra*, it is largely because of Rudrapatna Shamasastry (1868–1944). In 1905, Shamasastry discovered the manuscript of the *Arthashastra* in the library of Mysuru's Oriental Research Institute. References to the text existed but the manuscript itself had been lost. He published the Samskritam edition in 1909 and an English translation in 1915. Though other manuscripts have subsequently been discovered in other parts of the country, Shamasastry's name is interwoven with that of the *Arthashastra*. To return to Vatsyayana, Shamasastry took the issue seriously enough to write a paper on the presumed identification of Vatsyayana with Kautilya (Shamasastry 1917). Outside of Samskritam scholars and Indologists, this presumed identification between Vatsyayana and Kautilya may not be known. Consider those other names. Who was Mallanaga? This may or may not have been another name for Vatsyayana. Dramila might simply be a proper name, or it may mean the inhabitant of a specific geographical area—the south, the Dramila or Dravida region—of Bharatavarsha. Pakshilasvami was a logician, Vishnugupta was an astronomer and Angula was a mathematician. Despite being a figure of towering intellect, he could not have been all of these. In effect, Kautilya/Chanakya became almost a generic name, highlighting the revered and exalted position that came to be ascribed to him.

Despite a lot that has been written about him, including academic research, we don't know a great deal about the individual. There have been several books about Kautilya, especially in recent times. Let me quote from an earlier one, published in 1927.

> Throughout the whole of India, nitis or wise sayings attributed to him, are even now taught to beginners. This niti literature is not confined to India, but has travelled to distant countries like Ceylon, Burma, Tibet, Siam, and even to Persia and Arabia, and has found a place in the literatures of those countries.... The very fact that this almost universal adoration is paid to his memory, shows that Kautilya was in his own days regarded as a master, whose worldly wisdom and foresight gained for him the veneration of his contemporaries.... No authentic history of this remarkable man has reached us, except references to his success in diplomacy or proficiency in the Art of Government, of which he was a redoubtable exponent in the remote past. (Bandhyopadhyaya 1927)

Though it is difficult to sift fact from fiction, there is a tradition, and that is best encapsulated in the *Vishnu Purana*, which states the account as a prognosis for the future.

> Through the womb of a *shudra* woman, Mahanandi will have a son named Mahapadma Nanda. He will be extremely avaricious and extremely strong. As a destroyer of all the *kshatriya*s, he will be like another Parashurama. After him, the *shudra* kings will start to rule. Mahapadma will enjoy the earth as a universal emperor, with his commands not violated anywhere. He will have eight sons, Sumalya and others. Following Mahapadma, they will enjoy the earth. Mahapadma and his sons will be lords of the earth for one hundred years. After this, the *brahmana* Kautilya will uproot these nine Nandas. In their absence, the Mauryas will enjoy the earth. Chandragupta will be born and Kautilya will instate him. (Debroy 2022 [forthcoming])

That tradition has been restated in several texts—*Kathasaritsagara* (11th century CE) and *Mudrarakshasa* (4th to 8th century CE) are two examples. It is a tradition we are familiar with from film and television depictions. Chandragupta Maurya was crowned in 324 BCE or 321 BCE and accounts tell us about his being taught by Chanakya in Takshashila before the Nandas were ousted from Pataliputra. The Maurya empire lasted for a fairly long time, from Chandragupta Maurya to the assassination of Brihadratha around 180 BCE. In its heyday, it covered a large geographical area, with several regions incorporated as autonomous provinces. There was the royal capital in Pataliputra and there were four provinces, with provincial capitals in Tosali (for the east), Ujjain (for the west), Suvarnaigiri (for the south) and Takshashila (for the north). There was the civil service and the military. There was a system for municipal and village governance. There were principles for taxation, revenue generation and cross-border and internal trade and commerce. What were these and weren't these the principles stated in the *Arthashastra*?

As Sriram Balasubramanian states in his Introduction, he was sitting on the veranda of the Madras Sanskrit College and thinking about the *Arthashastra*, Adam Smith's *Wealth of Nations*, Angus Maddison's work and post-reform growth trajectories in India. To quote:

> Angus Maddison, the renowned economist and historian known for his work on the historical gross domestic product (GDP), showcased in his research that India and China were the leading economies (in terms of GDP and GDP per capita) in the world from 0 CE until the 17th century CE (Maddison 2001). Numerous historical accounts such as those by Alexander the Great, ancient Greeks such as Megasthenes, Chinese historian and traveller Fei Xin and the Seleucids (rulers of the erstwhile Hellenistic state from Western Asia) have all reiterated this in their writings. While some have analysed the reasons for India's economic dominance in this period, my intuitive view is that there had to have been a functioning ecosystem prior to 0 CE for

India to have been a superpower back then. There had to be a philosophical and economic framework that provided the springboard for almost a millennium of economic growth. Furthermore, this would also mean that the foundations of modern economic history attributed to Adam Smith's *The Wealth of Nations* can be predated by several centuries to individuals in the Indian subcontinent from an earlier era that was equally prosperous.

Adam Smith's 1776 magnum opus, *An Inquiry into the Nature and Causes of the Wealth of Nations*, is regarded as having established the modern discipline of economics. Though Smith's work is often equated with markets and the working of the individual hand, classical economists like him were much more conscious about institutions and their importance. After all, a market doesn't exist in isolation. It has a certain institutional and social context. One shouldn't forget that the father of economics wrote about moral sentiments before he wrote about the wealth of nations. Kautilya's work was about what would be called governance today.

There are notions of governance that have been developed by international organisations. The World Bank is an example. For instance, many years ago, in 1992 to be precise, the World Bank brought out a document seeking to link governance with development. This document offered the following definition of governance: 'Governance is defined as the manner in which power is exercised in the management of a country's economic and social resources for development.' Subsequently, the World Bank has produced a set of governance indicators to make cross-country comparisons and to benchmark a country's improvement over time. The organisation's set of governance indicators is based on six dimensions—voice and accountability, political stability and lack of violence, government effectiveness, regulatory quality, rule of law and control of corruption. As this listing makes obvious, we are talking about issues that are somewhat intangible. They are difficult to measure and quantify. Even if that was possible, data will be hard to come by, a task that becomes even more difficult because of the cross-country comparison that is being attempted. There is yet another problem, and that concerns the link between governance and economic development. Both governance and economic development need to be measured. And no matter how these two elusive concepts are measured, there is a correlation between them. As every statistician knows, correlation does not imply causation. Does better governance improve economic performance? Do better standards of living trigger citizen demand for better governance? Is there some other factor that provides the link between governance and economic development, leading to what statisticians call spurious correlation? Consider, for example, economic development measured by per capita income and the premium placed on a healthy environment. That premium clearly increases as per capita incomes increase but the relationship is a complicated one.

The author refers to both the Valmiki Ramayana and the Mahabharata and to specific instances from them.

Hast thou appointed to high offices ministers that are guileless and of well conduct for generations and above the common run? … Is any servant of thine, who hath accomplished well a particular business by the employment of special ability, disappointed in obtaining from thee a little more regard, and an increase of food and pay? I hope thou rewardest persons of learning and humility, and skill in every kind of knowledge with gifts of wealth and honour proportionate to their qualifications.… O lord of Earth, art thou equal unto all men, and can every one approach thee without fear, as if thou wert their mother and father? ... Do the accountants and clerks employed by thee in looking after thy income and expenditure, always appraise thee every day in the forenoon of thy income and expenditure? Dismissest thou without fault servants accomplished in business and popular and devoted to thy welfare? Are the agriculturists in thy kingdom contented? Are large tanks and lakes constructed all over thy kingdom at proper distances, without agriculture being in thy realm entirely dependent on the showers of heaven? Are the agriculturists in thy kingdom wanting in either seed or food? Grantest thou with kindness loans (of seed-grains) unto the tillers, taking only a fourth in excess of every measure by the hundred? O child, are the four professions of agriculture, trade, cattle-rearing, and lending at interest, carried on by honest men? Are thieves and robbers that sack thy town pursued by thy police over the even and uneven parts of thy kingdom? Consolest thou women and are they protected in thy realm? (Ganguli 2005)

This quote is from Sabha Parva of the Mahabharata. Just before the royal (rajasuya) sacrifice, Sage Narada arrives and asks Yudhishthira about the welfare of the kingdom. I have deliberately not quoted from my own translation,[1] but Kisari Mohan Ganguli's. That explains the slightly archaic English. There is a similar incident in the Valmiki Ramayana too, where Bharata is asked such questions by Rama, who is living in exile. The king's responsibility in that day and age is the government's responsibility today and that overall goal of governance hasn't changed. Narada or Rama may not have used the expressions 'inclusive growth' or 'Sabka Saath, Sabka Vikas', but the developmental goal of governance was precisely that. So, too, in the present. It will be no different in the future. The Mahabharata quote is a very good quote to illustrate both the objective of governance and some indication of economic welfare.

On the specifics of the measurement of governance, though not so much the definition, the focus is on what the government should do and on what the government fails to do satisfactorily. However, if that is what governance is about, we need not have coined a new word. The word government would have sufficed as a synonym for governance. The reason we have a separate word known as governance is because the two concepts are not identical. Governance is also about the process. It is also about decision-making. It is also about what is done by the citizens and by the community. It is

[1] Bibek Debroy's translation of the critical edition of the Mahabharata was published by Penguin Books in 10 volumes between 2010 and 2014 (with a box set in 2015).

much more than the delivery of public goods and services by the government. Perhaps, in the Indian context, one should use the plural word governments, because there is a three-tier structure of governance—the union government, state governments and local government. Governance is whose responsibility? The Preamble of the Indian Constitution begins with the words, 'We the People'. In other words, the responsibility for ensuring good governance, however defined, is not that of governments alone. The responsibility also devolves on citizens. That's the reason, in his recent 75th Independence Day speech, the prime minister referred not only to 'Sabka Saath, Sabka Vikas, Sabka Vishwas' but also to 'Sabka Prayas'.

Samskritam texts speak of dharma, artha, kama and moksha, the four objectives of human existence, the four purusharthas discussed by Sriram Balasubramanian. In the huge Samskritam corpus, there is much that is about dharma. There is an explanation that goes: यः धार्यते सः धर्मः. 'That which holds up is dharma.' Dharma holds up everything—dharma holds up society. But there are so many nuances to dharma. That is the reason that, in different contexts, dharma means moksha dharma (the dharma of liberation), good behaviour (better referred to as sadachara), raja dharma (the duty of kings), the dharma of the four varnas and ashramas and our own individual svadharma. At a certain level, governance is about dharma and, as this book brings out, it is not only about the government.

Today's government is what the king was then. Prithu was the first king. There are many possible words for king—nripa, bhupa, naradhipa, kshitisha. These are essentially synonyms but mean slightly different things. Nripa is short for 'nripati', lord of men. Bhupa is short for 'bhupati', lord of the earth. Naradhipa means lord of men while kshitisha means lord of the earth. But asked for a word for king, most people will probably think of raja, more accurately, rajan. Rajan, etymologically, is someone who gives delight. A king is known as rajan because his rule delights the subjects. There were kings before Prithu but none of them was a rajan. Prithu was the first rajan and, therefore, he is also referred to as the first king. These days, we expect a lot from the government—the government should do this, the government should do that. As individuals and as a community, we have abdicated our roles. That abdication only ensures bad governance. In that day and age, the king's role was limited—ensuring external and internal security, ensuring an efficient dispute resolution mechanism, punishing the wicked and protecting the virtuous. The rest of governance was ensured by individuals and the community. This comes across in our texts. This is also the picture painted in the *Arthashastra*. As a caricature, in a pure form of capitalism, which doesn't exist anywhere in the world, all decisions are taken by markets and individuals according to Adam Smith's invisible hand. As a caricature, in a pure form of socialism, which doesn't exist anywhere in the world, all decisions are taken by the state, the government. The Bharatiya template of dharma or governance offered a third alternative—some decisions were taken by individuals, some decisions were taken by the community, and some decisions were taken by the king/government. That comes across clearly in this volume.

We thus had a small number of tasks that the king or government was supposed to do and there were a set of tasks that individuals performed without the rod of individual or corporate social responsibility being invoked. The words 'ishta' and 'purti', often used together, are examples. Ishta can be translated as sacrifice but purti is best translated as civic works, and purti was undertaken because it was an individual's dharma to do so.

However, there was yet another layer between the individual and the king and that was the community or collective. More than anything else, it is this that has fallen into disuse. The government is forced to step in when there is a vacuum. Who ensured maximum retail price (MRP) was observed then? Who acted against unfair and restrictive business practices? There was no Competition Commission of India. The shrenis (guild is a bad word to use as translation) performed this task. The shrenis also ensured skill development. We didn't need the National Skill Development Corporation. We don't have to go back thousands of years. Even a couple of hundred will do. The British authored District Gazetteers. Initially, they did these for the country as a whole and then started ones that were specific to the districts. Let me cite the *Rohtak District Gazetteer* from the year 1883–1884. Around six years before this was written, there was a famine. To prevent famines from recurring, public waterworks were necessary in villages. The government of the day paid ₹25,000 in values of that time. The community contributed ₹45,000. There was a Police Reform Commission in 1901–1902 and its report is an illuminating account of how the village police system was worked by the community then. The District Gazetteers explain how one took care of many other things, as a community. Before we argue that we pay taxes so that the government performs these assorted tasks, the combined union and state government share of taxes is now 15per cent of GDP. The king of that day and age took one-sixth, roughly the same figure, as taxes.

I have mentioned that a lot has been written on Kautilya. While that's true, the bulk of that writing has been by historians and Indologists. It is only now that economists have started to probe Kautilya—L.N. Rangarajan, Balbir Singh Sihag, Satish Deodhar and now Sriram Balasubramanian. I hope for the day when an Indian version of Angus Maddison will work out the capital-output ratio of that age to be something like 4, and applying it to a tax/rate or savings rate of 16 per cent, justify the late Professor Raj Krishna's casual remark about 1–4 per cent rate of growth. If Damodar Dharmananda Kosambi could use coins to work out how fast money circulated, why not something like that too? The point is, as the author argues, that not enough research has been done.

The *Arthashastra* belongs to a broader template and corpus. In 2019, the official Economic Survey of India quoted both the *Arthashastra* and Kamandaka's *Nitisara*. Kamandaka, or Kamandakiya, described himself as a disciple of Vishnugupta's and extolled him. During this, he not only mentions the tradition of Chandragupta Maurya and Nanda but also says that Vishnugupta churned the ocean of the *Arthashastra* to produce the amrita of *Nitishastra*. The word 'artha' has the nuance of wealth generation while the word 'niti' has the nuance of good policy. Applied to the king, the latter is, of course, no different from raja dharma. But the dividing line between the two is thin. Many aphorisms attributed to Chanakya are not from the *Arthashastra* but Chanakya's *Raja-Niti*. An instance of this is a quote that is a favourite of finance ministers, the one about collecting taxes like a bee without damaging the flower. This is from *Raja-Niti*. Let me quote from Shamasastry's translation of the *Arthashastra*: 'This Arthasástra or Science of Polity has been made as a compendium of all those *Arthasástras* which, as a guidance to kings in acquiring and maintaining the earth, have been written by ancient teachers.'

The point is a simple one. There were earlier works on the *Arthashastra*, texts that didn't survive. Chanakya's work built on those and improved on those and was, in part, a bhashya, or commentary. Some authors preceded Chanakya and some succeeded him. The ones who preceded are called 'purvacharyas' by Kautilya and he was the most illustrious of them all. In any event, among those who followed, no one could match his intellectual prowess. As an extrapolation of the same point, the *Arthashastra* ideas exist not only in the text that has this name but also in Valmiki Ramayana, the Mahabharata (when Bhishma is lying down on his bed of arrows in Shanti Parva) and the *Dharmashastra* texts. This book has a fair amount of cross-referencing.

This volume also has a reference to P.V. Kane's mammoth work *History of Dharmashastra*. With the interest now being shown by economists, someday there will be a mammoth 'History of Arthashastra'. This interesting and readable book is just the beginning.

Bibek Debroy

Chairman, Economic Advisory Council to the Prime Minister

ACKNOWLEDGEMENTS

Grateful acknowledgement is made to the following for permission to reprint copyright material:

Balbir S. Sihag for tables from his book *Kautilya: The True Founder of Economics* published by Vitasta

L.N. Rangarajan for tables from his book *Kautilya: The Arthashastra* published by Penguin

Sumedha Verma for a map from 'Uttarapath and Dakshinapath: The Great Trade Routes of Jambudwipa' published by Swarajya

Professor Satish Deodhar, Dr Sushrutha S. and Karan Bhasin for co-authoring a section each with the author

1

Introduction

BACKGROUND

I was sitting on the veranda of the Madras Sanskrit College (MSC) with three things in front of me—Adam Smith's *Wealth of Nations*, a one-page summary of the *Arthashastra*, and the buzzing Chennai metropolis. Three things that seemed extremely unrelated somehow coalesced to get me thinking: Why is ancient Indian economic thought barely mentioned when talking about the Indian economy?

The Indian growth story after economic liberalisation in the 1990s has been one of the most discussed developmental success stories in the world. Rapid development in infrastructure and technology has powered this growth over the last few decades. Be it the mobile phones that we use, the expansive highways that we drive through or the enormous shopping malls that have engulfed our cities—all of this has transformed the way we live our lives for the better. Yet the emergence of India as a global power isn't a once-in-a-millennium event. Until its relatively recent decline in the Eighteenth century, it was a global economic powerhouse for several centuries. Angus Maddison, the renowned economist and historian known for his work on the historical gross domestic product (GDP), showcased in his research that India and China were the leading economies (in terms of GDP and GDP per capita) in the world from 0 CE until the 17th century CE (Maddison 2001). Numerous historical accounts such as those by Alexander the Great, ancient Greeks such as Megasthenes, Chinese historian and traveller Fei Xin and the Seleucids (rulers of the erstwhile Hellenistic state from Western Asia) have all reiterated this in their writings. While some have analysed the reasons for India's economic dominance in this period, my intuitive view is that there had to have been a functioning ecosystem prior to 0 CE for India to have been a superpower back then. There had to be a philosophical and economic framework that provided the springboard for almost a millennium of economic growth. Furthermore, this would also mean that the foundations of modern economic history attributed to Adam Smith's *The Wealth of Nations* can be predated by several centuries to individuals in the Indian subcontinent from an earlier era that was equally prosperous. Many other countries, Japan and China to name a few, who have a similar heritage have made efforts to document their past and learn from it. However, these questions were neither answered in history books that I was taught in my school nor the ones that I read later as an adult. It is no wonder then that I wasn't able to find any mention of ancient thought in our contemporary academic discourse on economics.

As I pondered over this question at the MSC, it dawned on me that I was holding a one-page summary of the *Arthashastra*. I decided to find an answer to this question. Since there hadn't been much work on ancient

Indian economic history, I was aware of the perseverance and effort that was needed for the task. I knew I might not find the exact answer I was looking for but I was convinced to begin the journey and see how it would unfold. Thus began an endeavour to explore the tenets of the *Arthashastra* that took over five years. A third-century BCE masterpiece, it details the various theories of statecraft, economics and social norms that were advocated by Kautilya, also known as Chanakya, who was the chief advisor to King Chandragupta Maurya. Containing detailed policy prescriptions, the work is divided into 15 books, over 150 chapters, 180 sections and 6,000 shlokas.

This journey has been exhilarating, to say the least. The numerous translations of Kautilya's *Arthashastra* were useful for understanding the geostrategic elements of the text, yet very little of it had explored the nuances of economic policymaking in a structured manner. 'Structure' is perhaps the biggest challenge in deciphering the *Arthashastra* and I realised that if one were to do that successfully, one needed to have understood modern economics and economic history, and also have cultural and linguistic knowledge of the subject. Moreover, I firmly believed that if one were to critique or analyse such a masterpiece, it was necessary to develop expertise in these areas to do justice to the text.

Given my background in economics, I was confident of the first criteria. I had always been fascinated by economic history because economics is a by-product of human interactions which is to an extent rooted in civilisational ethos. The modern economic thought is often so quantitatively driven that it is hard to get people to look beyond regressions and economic models. Many people tend to forget that no matter what the models say, it is the output of individual human interactions that eventually aggregates to form the macro-economy. I had been thinking along these lines since the global financial crisis of 2007-2009, which highlighted the fallibility of one-size-fits-all solutions. More fellow economists have acknowledged the need for more customised solutions to socio-economic problems. My research on the economics of happiness, well-being and inequality is an extension of this thinking.

On the second criteria, I was well versed in the cultural context. On the linguistic side, I was convinced that one had to have a reasonable knowledge of Samskritam[1] (संस्कृतं)—and read the text in the original Devanagari script. The poetic form of the text makes it impossible for the true nature of the text to be understood through a translation(s). This led me to the realisation that I had to refine my knowledge of Samskritam (I had done a part-time diploma from Madras Sanskrit College many years ago) to have a more comprehensive grasp of the subject. Besides taking additional courses, this pursuit led to interactions and discussions with a variety of Samskritam scholars, economists, historians, translators and even Indologists, all of whom brought various new perspectives on how to approach the subject. These experiences include driving almost three hours from Washington DC to

[1] The actual pronunciation of Sanskrit is Samskritam, hence we have adhered to it in the entire text.

New Jersey to participate in one of the annual Samskrita Bharati[2] events where individuals read, communicate and write Samskritam, and interacting with linguistic experts from across the globe. Though I have miles to go before mastering Samskritam, improvement in the language has been a great asset in my pursuit of understanding the *Arthashastra*.

Enhancing my expertise in these criteria is the primary reason why it has taken such a long time to write this book. I could have easily written a few Google-searched op-eds in news publications and compiled them into a book, pretending I knew everything but my conscience wouldn't have permitted me to do so. I have lived, breathed and experienced the text over the last five years, and such a beautiful journey is priceless in its purity. Much remains unexplored in the *Arthashastra* but using these skill sets, I have made a humble attempt to dive into Kautilya's brain to extract his ideas and highlight them in a structured manner.

BOOK OVERVIEW

The book aims to address three key things. First, it attempts to provide a structured interpretation of Kautilya's economic thought. Second, it seeks to contextualise it within the realm of contemporary economic trends and thought in India. Third, it tries to provide the common reader with insight into Kautilya's thinking in an easy-to-read yet comprehensive manner.

[2] For details visit https://www.samskritabharatiusa.org

This book attempts to look at Kautilya's thinking and its relevance today from a holistic perspective.

The first few chapters outline the big-picture ideas presented in the book followed by a perspective on ideas from the pre-Kautilyan era, an introduction to the *Arthashastra* (for the uninitiated) and a glimpse into the challenges in interpreting the text. The next chapters offer an overview of the philosophical frameworks that form the foundation of Kautilya's dharmic capitalism. The subsequent chapters deal with the three key elements of dharmic capitalism: wealth creation, sustainable growth and welfare, and a rule-based non-interventionist state. In wealth creation, some of the principles of trade that Kautilya used and their relevance today are discussed. Following this, the importance of gold in today's India and how Kautilya's ideas could be used to leverage this asset are elaborated upon. The next chapter deals with Kautilya's views on savings as an instrument of growth—something that is very relevant to the Indian economic story. Subsequently, Kautilya's views on sustainable growth and welfare through environmental, societal and familial responsibilities are explored. Furthermore, the concept of redistribution of wealth (as a consequence of inequality) in contemporary India is analysed and how Kautilya's ideas can be used to address it. The role of the rule-based yet non-intrusive state via the rule of law and enforcement of contracts in Kautilyan times and its relevance to today's times is looked into. Towards the end of the book, some areas of research that could be pursued to expand the scope of Kautilya's economic thinking are explored. The hope is that this book will provide a structure to understanding how Kautilya might have viewed today's challenges and addressed them.

RELEVANCE

One of the key explorations of this book is the *Arthashastra*'s relevance to today's economy. This is tricky to assess since it is highly subjective, depending on one's perspective and expertise. Furthermore, the large contextual differences between ancient times and today's world necessitate the need to extrapolate to bring the pieces together. Yet I think that these extrapolations are worth the stretch because they help to understand what Kautilya would have thought in today's times. This is similar to how economists try to interpret Adam Smith's views in the current context. In this backdrop, there are three broad questions that I have used to gauge this relevance:

1. What is the relevance of Kautilya's broad thematic economic principles/frameworks in today's times?
2. What is the relevance of the concepts used during Kautilya's times and their impact now?
3. As a consequence of the above-mentioned economic principles and concepts, how relevant is Kautilya's thinking to some of the contemporary solutions that we see today?

We deal with these questions at the end of the book. Instead of giving you the answers upfront, I thought it might be wise to allow you to make up your mind before

I give my assessment of this in the concluding chapters of the book.

THE AIM OF THE BOOK

Does this book provide a one-stop solution to all of India's economic problems? Not in the least. Does the book provide an empirically defined set of formulae and regression analysis that we economists love? Not really. Does the book provide a repartee of other ideological/ economic models that India has followed in the last few decades? No, because it focuses on the *Arthashastra*'s own merit. Does it hold up Kautilya as a flawless genius? No. However, it does perhaps suggest that despite his flaws, many of his ideas are relevant today.

The aim of the book is not to tell you that Kautilya is the only answer to all of the economic challenges that we face today. It certainly isn't the case but many of his ideas and philosophical constructs could help us in addressing some of our key challenges. The book aims to expand these ideas and philosophical constructs and also hopes to nudge the reader to appreciate the value of ancient economic thinking in contemporary discourse. The book deliberately doesn't take a judgemental view but rather highlights the linkages to today's economic themes and leaves it to the reader to decide what they make of it.

I owe a deep sense of gratitude to the three main translations of the text: R. Shamasastry's original translation (1915), T.G. Sastry's subsequent translation (1926) and the more recent three-volume series of R.P. Kangle (1965). Shamasastry's and Sastry's translations have been widely quoted in the various chapters of the book. I have no hesitation in saying that without these translations, the original text wouldn't have gained the limited traction that it has received among the masses. Furthermore, subsequent books on the *Arthashastra* by Rangarajan (*Kautilya: The Arthashastra* 1992), Dr K.S. Narayanacharya (*Relevance for Kautilya for Today* 2006), Balbir Singh Sihag (*Kautilya: The Founder of Economics* 2017) and Satish Deodhar (*Economic Sutra: Ancient Indian Antecedents to Economic Thought* 2019) have been extremely useful for my research and analysis. Professor Deodhar (IIM Ahmedabad) is a good friend and a co-author who has been very encouraging of my work on the subject. I must also convey my namaskarams (salutations) to Professor Balbir Sihag (a PhD in economics from the Massachusetts Institute of Technology and Emeritus Professor at the University of Massachusetts, Lowell) who is one of the finest minds I have ever met. The theoretical work that he has done on the subject and the various academic papers on Kautilya are a knowledge hub by themselves. His work, mentorship and his persona have been a motivational force for this book as well. The rest of the individuals whom I intend to thank are in the 'Acknowledgements' section of the book.

As a matter of full disclosure, I would like to mention that the work for the entire book, for over half a decade, was done in my personal capacity as an economist, economic history buff and author. These are views of the author(s) alone and do not represent the views/perspectives/policy prescriptions of the International Monetary Fund (IMF), its executive board, IMF management, the Independent Evaluation Office (IEO) or any other organisation. In simpler terms, these can't be attributed to the IMF or IEO or any of these organisations or entities in any form whatsoever and if quoted by media or other entities, there needs to be an *explicit* attribution to the personal views of the author and no one else.

All in all, at the end of the book, if you feel a sense of discovery of the Kautilyan perspective on the economy, contemplate on some of the ideas discussed and share them with your friends and family, I would then consider my book a success. After all, the message is more important than the messenger.

I hope you enjoy reading the book!

THE PRE-KAUTILYAN FIVE-PILLAR SUSTAINABLE MODEL[3]

Introduction

Kautilya was the protagonist of the Samskritam play *Mudrarakshasa* written circa sixth century CE by Visakhadatta (Abhyanker and Abhyanker 1916, 8). In that play, he was depicted as the prime minister of Emperor Chandragupta Maurya who had ruled India circa 300 BCE. Much later, from the book *Discovery of India* by Pandit Jawaharlal Nehru (1946), one got to know that Kautilya was not just an imagined protagonist of the play but an

[3] The following section is verbatim from the paper on which I collaborated with Professor Satish Deodhar from IIM, Ahmedabad, which was published as is by the European Historical Economics Society.

important historical figure. This changed understanding was possible because only a few decades prior to the publication of Nehru's book, concrete evidence that Kautilya was a historical figure had come to light. It was in the form of an old manuscript of Kautilya's *Arthashastra* that was discovered in Thanjavur, India. And subsequently, in 1965, Kangle wrote a sequential three-volume critical edition of the *Arthashastra* containing Samskritam text, translation and commentary, making it accessible to researchers globally.

In his treatise, Kautilya devoted his attention to the economic organisation of the state, the administrative setup, foreign relations, and the smooth continuity of a ruler. Several studies have been conducted in the recent past that throw light on Kautilya's contribution to global economic thinking much earlier than the likes of Adam Smith. For example, while Boesche (2003) has studied the *Arthashastra* from a political science perspective, Trautmann (2012) has covered the same from a historical and anthropological perspective. Importantly, Waldauer, Zahka and Pal (1996), as well as Skare (2013), Spengler (1971, 1980), Dasgupta (1993) and Sihag (2009, 2014) have also contributed to the literature from the perspectives of economists. These researchers cover Kautilya's prescriptions on trade, taxation, coinage, budget deficit, provision of public goods, market facilitation, wages and labour relations, property rights, internal and external security and several other topics.

In the first book of his treatise, Kautilya refers to the four-fold classifications of individuals' life objectives, life stages and life vocations. These are referred to as purusharthas (1.7.4), ashramas (1.3.9–12) and varnas

(1.3.5–8).[4] Purusharthas refer to dharma (righteous conduct), artha (material prosperity), kama (pleasure and love) and moksha (salvation). Among the purusharthas, Kautilya states that while there should not be excessive indulgence in any of the objectives, material prosperity is of foremost importance since other life objectives depend on it (1.7.6–7). In the context of the economic life of an individual, he states that a ruler should ensure the welfare of the people, for in the happiness of the subjects lies the happiness of the ruler (1.4.16, 1.19.34).

A seminal treatise like *Arthashastra* could not have been penned in circa 300 BCE as an abrupt one-off revelation. The contours of the Kautilyan worldview, by his own admission, were based on economic notions that had appeared in sacred and secular texts before his time. Terming his treatise as received knowledge, he gives due credit to his predecessors. For example, among others, Kautilya has made references to authors such as Brihaspati and Ushanas at least five times each. The treatises titled *Brihaspatya Shastra* and *Aushanasa Shastra* attributed to these two predecessors have been lost with time—or at least have not been rediscovered yet. While one finds passing references to Brihaspati in *Rig-Veda* as the purohita (preceptor) to King Indra and Ushanas in the Mahabharata as the purohita of the Asuras (Kangle 1965, Part III, 8, 42), Olivelle (2011, 174) confirms that most of the pre-Kautilyan political economy treatises have been lost.

[4] I have followed the notation (book.chapter.verse) to give a specific reference from any of the ancient treatises. The notation for the *Arthashastra* is from Kangle (1965).

This chapter attempts to scout and collate the ideas pertaining to economics in a coherent and structural manner, which reflects the sustainable economic model thesis of those times. These ideas have appeared interspersed in other Samskritam treatises, both the sacred and the secular, that predate Kautilya's *Arthashastra*, which evolved from the crucible of this literature. This is an attempt, to highlight the key tenets of the sustainable economic model. This model focuses on economic well-being through five key pillars, which, in modern terminology, are general well-being, sustainable wealth creation, market facilitation with private sector involvement, governance mechanisms through rule of law and state capacity for financial and economic transactions. These can be paraphrased into ideas of dharma, artha and kama from the purusharthas and the economic ideas of markets and governance from Vedic literature as well. These will be elaborated on in the following sections.

In this context, subsequent sub-sections would provide references to the summary of the purusharthas and related dimensions with their attendant economic implications in the society at that time. Moreover, they discuss economic well-being through the prism of dharma or righteous conduct and address the issue of economic governance of the state. Following these, aspects of wealth creation, namely artha and kama, and issues related to market facilitation, are covered in detail. Matters related to institutional capacity and financing of the state activities are also addressed followed by concluding observations.

The Purusharthas

Standard neoclassical economics describes utility maximisation as the only objective of life. The arguments of the utility function may be many, in terms of consumption of material goods and services, but the resultant maximised utility or satisfaction is unidimensional. However, recent advances in behavioural economics imply that human well-being, satisfaction or happiness is a multidimensional construct. This has been highlighted in the World Happiness Report (Helliwell, Layard and Sachs 2016) and the recent policy literature within major multilateral institutions (Balasubramanian 2017). In a multi-goal utility, deficiencies in or imbalances among different goals may lead to struggles and one may not live one's life to the fullest. There could be negative linkages among different goals of life which Frank (1999) defines as 'internality'. In a Gallup study conducted in 150 countries representing diverse cultures and ethnicities, five elements emerged that were associated with overall human well-being. These elements were related to career, social relations, financials, health and community well-being (Ghisellini and Chang 2018, 45–46). A similar proto-economic idea seems to have been expressed in ancient Indian literature where well-being is associated with a four-fold classification of purusharthas or life objectives, namely, dharma, artha, kama and moksha.

References to purusharthas appear in the two Samskritam epics, the Ramayana and the Mahabharata. These epics were written sequentially and much later than the *Rig-Veda*. Valmiki, the composer of the Ramayana (IIT Kanpur 2020) informs the readers early in the epic that he would like to convey the merits of purusharthas through his narration of the life story of King Rama (1.5.4). When Bharata goes to meet his brother Rama in the forest to give the news of their father's death, Rama advises Bharata not to overindulge in any of the three purusharthas—dharma, artha and kama (2.100.62–63, 73). Towards the end of the same epic, Kumbhakarna, the brother of the main villain Ravana, pleads to Ravana that one who follows the purusharthas appropriately would never face misfortunes in this world (6.63.9–11). Similarly, in the Mahabharata (Smith 2020), which covers the history of two warring cousins, the Kauravas and the Pandavas, the composer Vyasa mentions in the first book (1.56.33) and the last book (18.5.38) that concerning the four purusharthas, whatever is there in the Mahabharata may be found elsewhere, but whatever is not present there would not exist anywhere[5]. These are also referenced by socio-economic scholars in more recent times[6]. Given this historical context, among the purusharthas, we assert next that dharma constitutes an overarching principle for the sustainable economic model.

[5] The fourth purushartha, moksha, is not separately discussed in the Ramayana, the Mahabharata or the *Arthashastra* and is not the subject matter of this chapter as well. It is a metaphysical concept where the objective is to free one's soul from the cycle of birth and death and unite with the cosmic soul. A judicious conduct of the first three purusharthas may lead to moksha.

[6] Arise Bharat, 'Integral Humanism: Lectures of Deendayal Upadhyaya–1', Chapter 2. Available at https://arisebharat.com/2019/09/19/integral-humanism-lectures-of-deendayal-upadhyaya-2/

DHARMA—THE FOUNTAINHEAD OF WELFARE

The term dharma connotes moral values and ethical conduct. The earliest reference to dharma appears in *Rig-Veda* (Griffith 1886) in book 10, where the author invokes befriending Indra and requesting him to lead them into a righteous path (10.133.6). Later, both the Ramayana and the Mahabharata convey the dharmic choices that the protagonists of the epics must make in their lives. Although dharma as a life objective cannot be captured fully by economic theory, its comprehension can be attempted by stretching economic arguments and its attendant vocabulary. Economic theory assumes rational maximising behaviour on the part of an individual. Guided by self-interest, one is expected to maximise satisfaction (utility) or profit. Self-interest may account for an individual's desires; however, not all desired things by default qualify as desirable. What is desired may be free from ethical and moral commitments. As one moves through different stages of life, one's responsibilities change and therefore, one must condition one's desires accordingly. Dharma or righteous acts would be those that are desirable for different stages of life and which include the fulfilment of responsibilities encompassing moral and ethical standards. A student, a householder and a retired person would have different responsibilities. In fact, one's occupation also conditions one's righteous acts. For example, scientists from India's space research organisation, ISRO, may be sending missions to Mars; however, one will scarcely find them leading a flamboyant lifestyle. On the other hand, the head of a fashion and entertainment company might be in the limelight for his/her ostentatious way of life.

Economists have attempted to explain non-selfish interests as selfish ones. Boulding (1981, 6) pointed out that benevolence can be considered an example of self-interest. One's utility can increase when someone else becomes better off. This may explain charity as self-interest. Similarly, bequests and religious acts can also be construed as acts of self-interest as one can argue that utility is created out of the welfare of the offspring and the perceived enjoyment in the afterlife respectively. But then, to paraphrase Amartya Sen (1977, 322), one can define an individual's intentions in any such way that whatever he/she does is seen as furthering his/her self-interest in every isolated act of choice. Bowie and Simon (1977, 194–195) argue that if every act on the part of an individual can be explained as maximising behaviour out of self-interest, then the argument becomes futile.

Beyond self-interest, there are moral values that an individual possesses. Sen (1977, 326–327) has used the term 'commitment' to identify these moral values in a person. To paraphrase him again, if one were to see another person being tortured and that makes one sick and reach out, he/she acts out of sympathy. However, if one thinks that such action is wrong and hence one reaches out, one acts out of 'commitment'. This commitment points to ethical values and preferences arising out of principles rather than an act that increases one's utility. This is dharma or the righteous act. Shunning corruption only out of fear of law is not dharma. Shunning it as a matter of principle is dharma.

Not voting on election day is adharma. An individual vote perhaps may not change the results of an election; however, registering one's true preference is a democratic duty of a citizen and a dharmic act.

Kane (1941, 1–11) discusses various constituent elements of dharma in ancient literature. Among other things such as truthfulness, forthrightness and non-injury to other beings in thought, words and action, he also writes about charity as an act of dharma, which is mentioned in the Mahabharata. Ancient Indian society seemed to have developed a mature worldview on charity. We paraphrase here what the contributor of book 10 of the *Rig-Veda* had to say about charity (10.117.1–5): Death comes in various ways even to a well-fed person and riches come to her like the rolling of a cartwheel; hence, the rich should give alms to the poor who become her friends in future troubles.

Thus, not the sheer accumulation of wealth but the circulation of a part of it as a unilateral transfer within society was considered important by Vedic scholars. The *Bhagavad Gita* (Telang 1882), or simply *Gita*, which forms part of book six of the Mahabharata, describes right and wrong forms of daana (charity) in hymns 17.20 through 17.22. If charity is done for good causes and comes without any expectation of return, it is defined as sattvic (pure/good). If charity is ego-driven and given grudgingly with expectations, it is termed as rajas (given to passion), and if given with contempt to wrong causes and at wrong times, it is termed as tamas (ignorant, destructive).

In this context, there is a pertinent story in *Katha Upanishad* of the *Shukla Yajur-Veda* written circa tenth century BCE, regarding Sage Vajashravas giving all worldly possessions in alms (Müller 1879). Vajashravas's son, Nachiketa, points out to his father that while he had promised to give everything in alms, he should not be giving worthless alms in the form of aged cows who cannot even drink water, eat grass or give milk and are barren. To impress this point further, he asserts, 'Father, I am also your wealth. Whom are you going to give me to?' The conceited father tells Nachiketa in anger that he will give him to the deva of death, Yama. The story takes an interesting turn later; however, this narration gives an example of what rajas and/or tamas forms of charity could be.

While the above discussion about charity as a dharmic act does not formally convey the provision of meritorious goods or goods with positive externalities, the innate understanding of the social responsibility towards the needy in ancient India is quite evident. They highlight an individual's responsibility to enhance social and economic well-being within society. In addition to the individual's dharmic behaviour, ancient sages had also proposed an institutional framework for the collective good of the society; namely, the governance mechanisms for the state.

SOVEREIGNTY, GOVERNANCE AND WELFARE

If India's Saraswati–Sindhu civilisation dating back to the third millennium BCE has produced physical evidence of well-planned and fortified cities, use of trademarks and commercial links with far-off regions (Spengler 1971, 32; Moore and Reid 2008), her Vedic literature has also provided evidence of social organisation, a flourishing economy, and well-established political systems of governance. For example, numerous janapadas (republics) existed in the Vedic period from about 1200 BCE, concluding with the rise of sixteen mahajanapadas (great republics) by around 600 BCE (Singh 2008, 261). The description of different forms of political governance among these republics during this long period is mentioned in the Samskritam treatise *Aitareya-Brahmana* composed circa 800 BCE (Parpola 2007, 158). The descriptions include forms such as state (rajyam), great state (maharajyam), independent state (swarajyam), universal sovereign state (samrajyam) and a few others such as vairajyam (kingless republic). The names of many of the great republics, including, but not limited to, Magadha, Kosala and Gandhara (present-day Afghanistan), are extensively referred to in the Mahabharata.

In book three of the *Atharva-Veda* (Griffith 1895) it is mentioned that a king of a republic acquires the sublime power to govern by seeking cooperation from different sections of the society, chieftains and his own representatives (3.4). He derives the power to rule from his subjects who would support him, and the tribesmen would elect him for kingship. Even in the post-Vedic period, the coronation of a king was an offer of sovereignty by the people to the king. This was done by the representatives of the people called ratnis, who played a very important part in the investiture of the king (Ambedkar 1946, 1.6.4). One could call this arrangement in modern economic terminology as upholding the 'social contract' theory. Early Buddhist literature also seems to uphold this social contract theory, where the king is the chosen leader of his people, selected by them to ensure property rights and security (Dasgupta 1993, 20). Since kings in these republics derived their power to rule from their subjects who would support them to become kings, the rulers were bound to have economic policies for the welfare of their subjects. Kautilya's emphasis on material prosperity and his advice that the ruler's happiness lies in ensuring the welfare of the people seems to emanate from this very idea.

Emphasis on societal welfare had found expression in Vedic literature much earlier than that in the *Arthashastra*. Knapp (2006, 1) refers to the famous Vedic verse, 'May all be happy, may all be free from disease, may all realise what is good, and may none be subject to misery.' Specific examples of this ideal appear in the epics. In the Ramayana (IITK 2020), when Bharata, the brother of King Rama, visits him in the forest, Rama advises Bharata to follow policies that have a maximum societal benefit and minimum cost and to ensure that the implementation of this policy does not get delayed (2.100.19). He tells Bharata to appoint wise persons for policy formulation, for one wise person is of greater help than soliciting 1,000 fools (2.100.22–24). On Rama's return to Ayodhya after fourteen years of banishment and vanquishing Ravana, Bharata informs Rama that he had taken good care of the kingdom in his absence and that the towns, treasury, granaries and army had increased tenfold in fourteen years (6.127.55). And, in the Mahabharata, Bhishma the grand old patriarch of the Kuru clan, as well as Sage Narada, give similar advice to King Yudhishthira regarding features of their welfare state (Deodhar 2019, 43–50).

The role of dharma for an individual and the role of governance mechanisms for the state served as the foundational elements to accelerate economic progress. Between these two lie the aspects of wealth creation, pleasure-seeking, market facilitation, and creation of state capacity through money and public finance.

ARTHA AND KAMA—SEEKING WORLDLY PLEASURE

Ancient Indian literature corroborates the notion that celebrating life through acquiring wealth and pleasure and love was a part of an individual's purushartha. There are many hymns in the *Rig-Veda* (Griffiths 1886) that capture matters related to desires, material prosperity, wealth and interest rate. For example, in book 9 there is a narration on how we should follow our desires and wealth (9.112.1–4). To paraphrase, it reads:

> We all have a variety of hopes and plans. We strive for wealth in different ways. We follow our desires like cows follow one another. The male desires a female's approach. A frog looks forward to a flood, an arrow smith seeks someone who will pay him in gold, a craftsman seeks something that is to be restored and a priest seeks worshippers.

That a purohit also desires worshippers is a very witty observation indeed. Further, in book 2, the author requests Indra to provide the best of riches, capable minds, pleasant weather and a sweet speech (2.21.6). Yet another Vedic prayer called 'Chamakam' ('This and That') repeatedly seeks in a rhythmic tone, material objects, happiness, power, knowledge as well as spiritual well-being (Nadkarni 2012). In the *Rig-Veda*, there are also descriptions of a young man wearing a high-quality robe (3.8.4) and Varuna deva wearing a shining golden robe (1.25.13). It also contains a devotional prayer sung in praise of Lakshmi, the goddess of wealth. Known as the 'Shri Sukta', this prayer seeks fertility and prosperity from Lakshmi. Similarly, in the *Atharva-Veda* (Griffith 1895), a householder seeks benediction on a newly built house that is teeming with family members, delicious food preparations and cattle and horses (3.12). These hymns are the expressions of a strong desire for a prosperous life on earth for the people. They also express learnings from difficult moments in one's life. For example, in the 'Dice' hymn of the *Rig-Veda*, the seer laments alienating his wife and property to gambling and advises that one should take up farming to make money because real enjoyment is in the wealth that is acquired through toil(10.34.1–14).

One also finds an example of bargaining between a buyer and a seller in the *Rig-Veda*. In book 4, the concept of reservation prices gets referred to, though, of course, modern formal economic terms are not used. It is interesting to note that a devotee is shown trying to save cost even in a transaction for buying offerings for the devas (4.24.9–10). I paraphrase this bargaining below:

> A devotee is trying to buy nectar (soma) and fried barley from a priest (purohit) as sacrificial offerings to seek Indra's favour. The devotee (buyer) bids a low price and the offerings remain unsold, for the purohit (seller) is not ready to accept the low price. The offerings cannot be sold for a mere price of ten cows. The needy buyer and shrewd seller both milk out the udder (i.e., bargain hard for the price).

This description tells us that the quotes of the buyer's bid price and seller's offer price are expressed in terms of the number of cows and that the reservation price of the seller was higher than ten cows.

Furthermore, in book 2 of the Mahabharata (Smith 2020) after the Great War has been won, Arjuna forcefully counsels Yudhishthira to occupy the throne and give up the thought of becoming a mendicant. Among other things, he counsels him that religious acts, pleasures, joy, courage, wrath, learning and a sense of dignity all proceed from wealth. Moreover, he tells him that wealth brings about the accession of more wealth, the way domesticated elephants are used to capture their wild counterparts (12.8.1–37). The expression that wealth brings about further accession of wealth seems to capture the importance of capital as an input to create more wealth. It is worth mentioning that Kautilya borrows the same example of elephants in the *Arthashastra* to underscore the point that capital begets capital (9.4.27).

A reference to charging interest on capital will be quite appropriate here. In the Indian tradition, debt (rna) and its repayment have often been mentioned in the *Rig-Veda* but whether interest was charged is not clear (MacDonnell and Keith 1912). However, by 700 BCE, Panini the grammarian had laid down rules and symbols for expressing interest in percentage terms (Datta 1927). In fact, even the daily and monthly compounding of interest had been worked out. A grammarian only systematises what is socially prevalent. Hence, expressing interest as a percentage of debt must have been known to Indians circa 700 BCE. Dharmashastras written after Panini's grammar confirm that moneylending and charging interest was considered a legitimate activity (Jain 1929). It is no surprise then that Kautilya had gone a step further in the *Arthashastra* (Kangle 1965), prescribing varying interest rates depending upon the risk involved (3.11.1, 5.3.43, 7.11.17, 7.12.20–27).

Apart from the acquisition of material wealth, kama or pleasure and love was also a life objective that was sought after. According to Kane (1941, 8), this included sexual, emotional and artistic expressions. Panini makes a mention of the treatises called *Nata Sutras (Aphorisms for Actors)* belonging to two schools of performing arts attributed to the Vedic branches of Krashashwa and Shilalin[7] (Mehta 1999, xxiv). These developments had occurred at least a few centuries before Kautilya wrote the *Arthashastra*. And later, sometime between 200 BCE and 200 CE, Bharata Muni would go on to write the

[7] These were Vedic sages who had made the Nata Sutras.

Natyashastra (*Science of Dramatics*) and Vatsyanana would write the *Kama Sutra*.

It is pertinent to mention that in the *Arthashastra*, Kautilya gave details about the functioning of the superintendent of courtesans (2.27.1, 26, 28). The superintendent was expected to appoint a courtesan for 1,000 panas at an entertainment establishment. Moreover, he was supposed to pay maintenance to the teacher who imparts knowledge of various performing arts such as singing, acting, dancing, writing and playing musical instruments.

India has had a wide range of philosophical traditions including the atheist schools of thought which fall outside of Vedic traditions. Billington (1997, 43) affirms that in the sixth century BCE, a philosopher named Charvak founded and advocated the materialist school called Lokayat. The followers of this tradition are sometimes known as Charvaks. Charvak is famously quoted to have said, 'As long as you live, live happily. Drink ghee [clarified butter] even if you may have to borrow money. For, once consigned to flames [after death], who can return [to enjoy life]?'

Clearly, he talked about enjoying material prosperity and pleasures in this life and gave primacy to artha and kama over dharma and moksha. A few of his other maxims are, 'Rather a pigeon today than a peacock tomorrow' and 'A sure piece of shell is better than a doubtful coin of gold.' T. Mahadevan (1960, 66) summarises these maxims as rephrased idioms in modern English—a bird in hand is worth two in the bush. Nagarjuna Rao (1970, 29), strikes a cautious note, saying that svecchavihara (licence) to do anything and everything is not the same as swatantrya (freedom) and that this common-sense hedonism was an oversimplification and a unidirectional theory of ethics. All in all, a focus on the need to prosper materialistically is undeniable. The dynamics of the actual fulfilment of artha and kama were facilitated by the government through infrastructure construction and the provision of market mechanisms for labour, goods and services in the private sector.

Infrastructure and Markets

Both in the Ramayana and the Mahabharata, there are references to the advice given to kings for the provision of the public good. While Rama is leaving for a fourteen-year-long banishment from the kingdom, he advises Bharata to make sure that the kingdom has enough public places for citizens, potable water tanks for travellers and reservoirs for farmers so that they do not have to depend entirely on the rains (2.100.43–45). The construction of such public works does not seem to be mere imaginary descriptions since one also finds details of the process of road construction (2.80.1–22). Similarly, in book 2 of the Mahabharata, Sage Narada articulates his concern for public works when he asks whether large water tanks and lakes have been constructed at periodic distances to tackle water scarcity in the rain-fed areas of the country (2.5). He also reminds Yudhishthira about the fatherly duties of a king—taking care of the blind, the dumb, the lame, the deformed, the friendless and the ascetics who have no homes. Kautilya refers to all these issues in his treatise too (2.1.19–20, 26).

Narada mentions that there are four commercial market activities (vaarta)—namely, agriculture, trade and commerce, animal husbandry and lending at interest, which lead to the economic welfare of the people. For carrying out these market activities unhindered, he asks Yudhishthira if he is alert to internal security by apprehending robbers and ensuring the coordination of officers looking after agriculture, city, citadels, merchants and law enforcement. Moreover, he asks whether the king helps farmers by extending loans for seedlings at a rate not exceeding one-fourth of the produce. Narada also hopes that merchants coming from faraway places are treated fairly and only just dues are collected from them. Thus, Narada alerts Yudhishthira to his important role in market facilitation. In book 2 of the *Arthashastra*, Kautilya elaborates on similar activities and responsibilities of the state (2.4.9–16, 2.16.11, 2.21.31).

The *Shukla Yajur-Veda* (Griffith 1899), written circa 1000 BCE, has given an exhaustive list of labour professions in chapters 16 and 30 (30.1–22, 16.1–147). They include vocations ranging from acrobats to astrologers, basket-makers to butchers, carpenters to charioteers, dyers to drummers, horse hostlers to hunters, physicians to purohits, weavers to warriors, jewellers, goldsmiths, dancers, elephant keepers and many more. The hymns pay homage to these professionals (Pathak 2018b, 117). In the Ramayana too, a detailed list of professions is given in the context of road construction activity (2.80.1–22), which includes skilled vocations such as land surveyors, land plotters, diggers, mechanical operators and many others. Rama advises Bharata that there should not be any delay in paying bread or wages to service providers, for otherwise they get incensed, which may cause corruption to set in (2.100.33). Similar advice appears in the Mahabharata, where Sage Narada advises King Yudhishthira that payments to artisans are never to be delayed beyond four months and that there are no arrears to payments made to soldiers (2.5.).

The professions mentioned above had evolved into well-organised guilds that facilitated economic and trade-related activities. The guilds were variously called shreni, sangha, nikaya and nigama. The heads of the guilds and prominent professionals were given honorific titles such as shreshtha or jyesthaka (Pathak 2018b, 121). Kings took their help in the management of finances, on trade-related matters and even sought finances for public buildings and army operations. Shreshthas would be deputed by kings to exercise authority on their behalf (Mukerji 1963, 229). Building on these developments, we observe that Kautilya wrote an entire chapter in the *Arthashastra* detailing the management of labour laws and labour unions by the judges (3.14.1–37).

In the Vedic and post-Vedic ages, while land was cultivated individually, it had acquired a sacred status since land was considered a goddess (Kazanas 2010, 16–17). Various words suggestive of material prosperity or wealth are mentioned in the Vedic hymns, including gold, jewels, horses, cattle and elephants. However, land is never mentioned as wealth. The Samskritam names for the earth, Vasudha and Vasundhara, mean 'wealth-producing' and 'wealth-holding' respectively, indicating that land is a source of material wealth and not wealth in itself. Kazanas (2010, 41) reports that as per Jaimini's *Purva Mimamsa*, a treatise on Indian philosophical systems written circa fourth century BCE, the earth belonged to all beings and the right to property was not vested in the king. His kingly power was only to govern the realm. This is in contrast to the principle of eminent domain which thrusts the ownership of land upon deva and the king as his representative on the earth. Since the king did not enjoy eminent domain on land, this facilitated the emergence of the concept of private property over time. Over many generations, when families continued to hold and till specific parts of the land, vested private interests were created and the rights of alienation came to be recognised (Majumdar 1922; Madan 1981). By the fourth century BCE, the state had recognised movable and immovable property rights. Kautilya's detailed writing on the state's laws on protecting land ownership, charging land revenue and buying and selling of land in book 3 of the *Arthashastra* seems to be a continuation of the state's policy of protection of private property, including land (3.9.1–38).

State Capacity Through Money and Finance

Provision of public goods, market facilitation and state administration cannot continue unless rulers can value goods and services in monetary terms and have a reasonable system of revenue generation and its judicious use. There are quite a few references that show that punch-marked coins and unstamped metallic currency were used as money much before the Kautilyan era. For example, in the *Rig-Veda*, the poet praises the munificence of his patron king for paying him 100 nishkas or gold coins (1.126.2). That the nishkas were gold coins is affirmed by the definition of coins given by Panini (Bhandarkar 1921). Besides this, the *Rig-Veda* refers to unstamped metallic currency or the hiranyapinda—bullion beaten into a definite shape (Das 1925, 39). Bhandarkar (1921) also quotes from the Buddhist Jataka tales, where nishkas are referred to as gold coins, and that the other kinds of coins made of silver and copper were called karshapana. Later, Kautilya gives an elaborate list of wages and salaries for different professions which are expressed in terms of the panas, a punch-marked coin of his times (5.3.1). He also gives detailed directions in book 2 regarding a mint master's responsibilities in minting coins such as panas, half pana, quarter pana and so on with specified contents of metals such as silver, copper, lead, iron, tin and antimony (2.12.24).

The *Rig-Veda* also mentions subjects paying taxes. S. Chitrav (1998) points out that book 10 refers to subjects expected to pay taxes (bali) and tributes to the king (10.173.6). This idea is developed much further in the Mahabharata. In book 12 of the epic, Bhishma, the grand old patriarch of the Kuru clan, advises King Yudhishthira on taxation (12.88). Below is an excerpt translated by Ganguli (1896):

> A king should milk his kingdom like a bee gathering honey from plants. He should act like the keeper of a

> cow who draws milk from her without boring her udders and without starving the calf. The king should (in the matter of taxes) act like the leech drawing blood mildly. He should conduct himself towards his subjects like a tigress in the matter of carrying her cubs, touching them with her teeth but never piercing them therewith. He should behave like a mouse which though possessed of sharp and pointed teeth still cuts the feet of sleeping animals in such a manner that they do not at all become conscious of it. A little by little should be taken from a growing subject and by this means should he be shorn. The demand should then be increased gradually till what is taken assumes a fair proportion. The king should enhance the burthens of his subjects gradually like a person gradually increasing the burthens of a young bullock. Acting with care and mildness, he should at last put the reins on them.

This idea about taxation was later endorsed by Kautilya in the *Arthashastra*. He opines in book 5 of his treatise that taxes should be collected sustainably just as only the ripened fruits are picked from the orchards and the unripe ones are given time to mature (5.2.70). These kinds of advice given by ancient Indian thinkers remind us of a similar view expressed by Jean-Baptiste Colbert (McKechnie 1896, 77)—albeit two millennia later—that the art of taxation consists in so plucking the goose as to procure the largest quantity of feathers with the least possible amount of hissing.

While tax and tax revenue are generic terms, their sources are clearly identified in the epics. Land and commerce were the two main sources of revenue for the state then; there were seven types of prevalent taxes. First was the land tax, a fixed proportion of the produce demanded by the king. The second was a tax called gomis on animal husbandry, which was a charge on cattle breeding and cattle used as a means of conveyance for commodity trade. Gomis was a term for Banjaras, who kept large numbers of bullocks, donkeys and mules. They were taxed lightly due to their importance in the movement of goods. The third was a shulka, which was equivalent to the customs duty of modern times. The fourth and fifth types were taxes on salt mines and pans and other mined materials. The sixth was the toll on river crossings and the seventh was a tax on elephants. The elephants belonged to the state and no one could capture and use them without permission (Gokhale 2018, 104–108). Later, Kautilya identified seven sources of revenue and more than ten types of taxes (Mahulikar 2018, 129–133).

Prudence in the use of tax revenue has been stated in the ancient texts. In book 2 of the Mahabharata, Narada makes Yudhishthira aware of his various duties as a king (2.5.). Among many others, he alerts the king about financial prudence by asking whether his expenditures are about a fourth, third or, at worst, half of his income, and whether his accountants appraise him on his income and expenditure every forenoon. Once again, Kautilya carries this idea further. In book 5 of the *Arthashastra*, Kautilya categorically mentions that the wages and salaries of government servants should not exceed 25 per cent of the total revenue (5.3.1). These two pieces of advice remind one of the modern concepts of the state completely avoiding revenue deficit.

Concluding Comments

Several researchers have looked into the contributions made by Kautilya's *Arthashastra*. By his own admission, it was received knowledge that he systematised and elaborated on. While Kautilya makes mention of at least two of his predecessors, Brihaspati and Ushanas, their works seem to have been lost over time. Though the works specific to these predecessors are not available, one does find threads of Kautilya's writings in many other ancient sacred and secular texts. The expressions of pre-Kautilyan proto-economic thought across many Samskritam treatises were grounded in their socio-cultural and material environment. Though disjointed and scattered in different texts, these thoughts were profound for their times. The *Arthashastra* must be viewed, therefore, as an amalgamation of proto-economic thoughts that evolved in the crucible of the Vedic and post-Vedic Samskritam literature.

In this chapter, we have attempted to structure these thoughts into a sustainable economic model with a five-pillar approach. The importance of economic and social well-being in modern times has been characterised by the pillar of dharma while the citizens' collective responsibilities have been exemplified by the pillar of governance. The idea of wealth creation and pleasure-seeking, propounded by Kautilya as well as modern economic thinkers, has been highlighted in pre-Kautilyan texts by the artha and kama pillar. The pillar of market facilitation for land, labour and goods has been highlighted extensively in texts such as the Ramayana, the Mahabharata and Vedic literature.

Furthermore, the last pillar of institutional capacity has been articulated through the lens of money creation, taxation and public finance in many of these relevant texts. Suffice to say that the five-pillar economic model has been highlighted in the *Arthashastra* in various places and has been conceptualised in modern economic thought as well. In this chapter, we highlighted the origins of these ideas and their corresponding economic applications in ancient India.

The pre-Kautilyan literature described here can be considered as the pre-eminent, early pre-classical literature on economic thought. While otherworldly features of Indian tradition may be unique, this chapter shows that broad proto-economic principles and their subsequent economic models were used as political economy tools in ancient India. Ingram (1919) said, 'Institutions must be judged in their proper setting of time and place, and men cannot be understood unless they are brought into connection with the life of their own country and their own age.' In this context, the similes on taxation in terms of flowers and honeybees, capital growth in terms of wild and domesticated elephants, the uncertainty of riches in terms of a cartwheel and desires in terms of a frog's craving for rains seem extraordinary. Similarly, the concept of purusharthas and other ancient Indian texts seems to resonate with the ideas mooted in modern-day theories of sustainable and behavioural economics. It was important to talk about these before delving into the text of the *Arthashastra* in detail in subsequent chapters.

2

An Overview of the *Arthashastra*—Questions, Answers and Translations

QUESTIONS AND ANSWERS

This chapter tries to summarise the *Arthashastra* in simple terms for the reader who doesn't have prior knowledge of the subject. The hope is that the questions and answers give the reader the necessary background information. Besides providing information, one hopes that it helps to place the *Arthashastra* in the context of seminal contemporary texts.

What Is the *Arthashastra*?

The *Arthashastra* is a third century BCE masterpiece that details the various theories of statecraft, economics and social norms that were advocated by Kautilya, the chief advisor to King Chandragupta Maurya. The text provides an overview of geostrategic, economic and political strategies and policies that were adopted by the Mauryan Empire. Detailed policy prescriptions are given in the 15 books, 150 chapters, 180 sections and 6,000 shlokas in the text. The chapters are thematically segregated and were used as a foundation for policymaking in those times.

How Big Was the Mauryan Kingdom during Chandragupta Maurya's Rule?

The Mauryan dynasty occupied large sections of contemporary India from 321 BCE to 185 BCE and was one of the first dynasties to have a pan-Indian presence[1]. The timeline of the key Mauryan leaders is shown in Table 2.1 for further reference.

TABLE 2.1: *Timeline of the Mauryan Rulers*

Ruler	*Span of Rule*
Chandragupta Maurya	321–297 BC
Bindusara	297–272 BC
Ashoka	272–232 BC
Dasaratha	232–224 BC
Samprati	224–215 BC
Salisuka	215–202 BC
Devavarman	202–195 BC
Satadhanvan	195–187 BC
Brihadratha	187–185 BC

The Mauryans, at their peak, conquered much of current central and northern India, including parts of contemporary Iran as shown in Map 2.1. Chandragupta Maurya initially conquered Pataliputra and by 321 BCE had captured much of the north-western part of contemporary India. Following the victory in the Seleucid–Mauryan War (which started around 305 BCE), he is said to have captured Gandhara (Afghanistan), the Hindu Kush and parts of eastern

[1] https//www.nationalgeographic.org/encyclopedia/mauryan-empire/

Iran. In subsequent battles, he also went south of the Vindhyas (southern India in today's geography) to dominate the southern Deccan plains. At the peak of his powers, he had one of the largest empires in the world.

MAP 2.1: *Mauryan Kingdom during Chandragupta Maurya's Time—300 BCE*

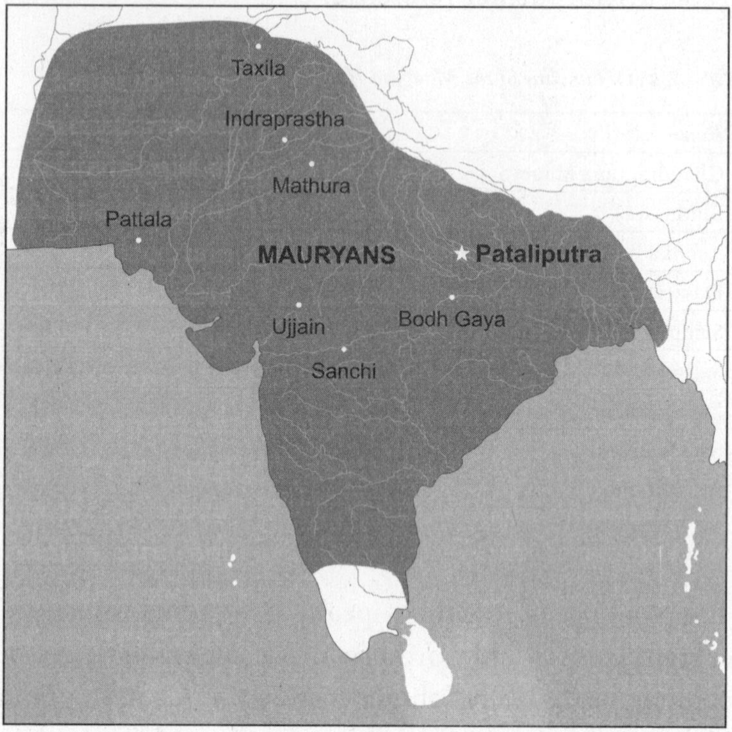

Source: Wikimedia Commons

What Are Some of the Topics that the *Arthashastra* Deals With?

This text deals with a variety of topics including foreign policy, economics, state administration, law and justice, defence and war, among others. Parallels can be drawn between them and contemporary ideas that address some of the socio-economic challenges of our time. For example, the six-fold foreign policy strategy has been well researched and used in several contemporary foreign policy discussions in India and other countries. Other key principles on taxation, trade, inequality, and debt sustainability are highlighted in the *Arthashastra*.

Why Aren't There Many Direct Interpretations of the Original Text? How Complex Is It?

There aren't many interpretations because of a few reasons. First, the text itself is in dense Samskritam and requires a detailed understanding of both the language and its socio-economic/political nuances. In that sense, even the currently available interpretations—by Shamasastry (1915), Kangle (1965) and Rangarajan (1992)—are bound to evolve as we discover more of the text and understand its contextual nuances. The original interpretation by Shamasastry (1915) is one of the most authentic in my opinion. Without the ingenuity of Shamasastry, this text wouldn't have been discovered in the first place. Second, the chapters by themselves seem to be in silos of sorts for the modern reader, though we detail why it's framed this way in the translations sub-section. They have been classified in a way where ideas (or a combination of ideas) in a particular chapter are relevant to understanding other chapters in the text. In that sense, creating a coherent framework becomes a challenge since it requires a detailed compilation of ideas extracted from individual chapters. Third, the combination of dense language and the intermingling of themes across chapters makes it challenging to create a coherent framework that can do justice to Kautilya's vision.

What Are Some of the Recent Interpretations by Contemporary Writers?

Much of the literature on Kautilya focuses on his views related to foreign policy and state administration. Many researchers (Saran 2018) have also looked at the geo-political dimensions of Kautilya's views. These also cover a wide range of issues in state administration among others. Kautilya's views have also been used as business and self-help ideas (Pillai 2019) that have gained popularity among the masses. Furthermore, there have been also many fictional interpretations (Sanghi 2012) of Kautilya that have captured the imagination of many readers.

Does the *Arthashastra* Cover All that Is Available Today in Economic Policymaking?

Even the most ardent admirer of Kautilya would agree that the *Arthashastra* doesn't constitute all of today's policymaking ideas and theories found in economic textbooks. However, it does provide a comprehensive set of ideas that serve as foundations for many macroeconomic concepts and remain relevant in contemporary times. These ideas are often attributed to Adam Smith's *Wealth of Nations* in contemporary economic discourse, but some of us feel otherwise. Excellent books, like

B.S. Sihag's *Kautilya: The True Founder of Modern Economics*, focus on the theoretical basis for Kautilya to be the pre-eminent thinker of economic ideas much before the likes of Adam Smith.

Was Kautilya the Originator of These Ideas in the *Arthashastra* or Did He Compile Them from Pre-eminent Works before His Time?

Kautilya himself admits that some of his ideas were inspired by historical works such as the Ramayana and the Mahabharata among others. In a paper with Deodhar (2020), I have articulated how our purusharthas, Vedas and Puranic texts have many tenets of economic thinking before Kautilya. While his ideas are a conglomeration of erstwhile texts, Kautilya also provides a personalised touch to the *Arthashastra*, with his ideas and perspectives. So yes, Kautilya wasn't the sole originator of these ideas but he was the closest to bring them together in an appropriate form (though it is still far from a modern framework) during his time.

Was He More of a Strategic Geopolitical Thinker or a Political Economist?

This question forms the core of this book. Much of the discourse has been on Kautilya's views on geopolitics but there seems to be an inherent political economist driving it. Unlike his contemporaries, Kautilya seems to have kept economics as a foundation for the geopolitical progress of his kingdom. Even the title of the *Arthashastra* has artha (wealth) as its central theme, not something like defence (raksha) or state (rajya). In that sense, while he is perceived as a strategic geopolitical thinker, in reality he was a political economist who viewed economics as a means to achieve prosperity and geopolitical expansion.

What Is His Legacy Compared to Other Historical Political Thinkers?

His legacy is often viewed through the lens of contemporary Western thinkers. Much of the literature suggests that there was a Machiavellian streak to him and that his geopolitical strategies (which includes spying and other questionable practices) take centre stage. There are three distinct reasons why I disagree with this comparison. First, the intentions of both authors are very different. As mentioned by Ray in his 1999 book, *Tradition and Innovation in Indian Political Thought*, Machiavelli's primary purpose was to maintain the rule of the king. Kautilya, on the other hand, has explicitly mentioned many a time that the main purpose of the text is the 'yogakshema' and 'rakshana' of the subjects, that is, the welfare, protection, and administration of the people. Rarely does one find Kautilya glorifying the king, his personality, or his rule in isolation—even in instances where he talks about political power, the main purpose is to benefit the people. This is in direct contrast to the Machiavellian text, *The Prince*, given that the *Arthashastra* is written through a different lens. Second, the comparison with

Machiavelli falls short when viewed through an economic lens. Many of the comparisons should be along the lines of ancient economic thinkers such as Adam Smith and Jules Dupuit. This has been illustrated in detail in Table 2.2.

TABLE 2.2: *A Comparative Analysis on the Requirements and Origins of Economics*

Requirements proposed by	*Characterization of Economics as a Science*	*Kautilya's* Arthashastra *3rd–4th Century BCE*	*Adam Smith's* The Wealth of Nations *1776*	*Dupuit and Other Engineers 1830-1870*
Groenewegen	Definition	Broad like today	Narrow	Narrower
	Scope	Broad like today	Narrow	Narrower
Spiegel	Separate	Yes	No	
Marshall	Writing a treatise	Yes	Yes	No
Barber, Dupuit, Landretb and Colander	Number of concepts	Reasonable	Reasonable	Very few
	Original	Many	Just one or two	A few
	Synthesis	Yes	Yes	No
	Consistent	Yes	Not always	Yes
Schumpeter	Economy as a system	Yes	Yes	No
	Method or tooled knowledge	Scientific	Pre-scientific	Scientific

Source: Sihag 2014

Third, the narrative on Kautilya is not easily comparable with other individuals in different eras primarily because of the diversity and complexity of ruling such a vast area of land. Moreover, the socio-cultural dynamics of Kautilya's time are very different to that of the Western world. In that context, comparisons with other historical political thinkers are often an opportunistic but futile exercise. Furthermore, India's economic survey conducted in 2020 has an interesting box item that reinforces this misaligned comparison with Machiavelli and also compares his thinking with Aristotle and Adam Smith.

What is the Value Addition that Kautilya Brings to Economic Thinking Compared to Other Economic Thinkers?

In my view, his biggest value addition was the emphasis on sustainable and equitable wealth creation through innovative ideas that were flexible enough to suit large sections of the population. Given that the capital of the Mauryan dynasty was one of the largest cities in the world, his ideas had a wide reach and impact. It also provided a large sample size to determine the success of some of his policies unlike other thinkers who were either academic or philosophical (Adam Smith). In that sense, Kautilya was the earliest policy economist who could implement futuristic policies at scale with great flexibility. The vision of involving the private sector, the role of a limited yet rule-binding state along with the ideals of dharmic capitalism (which we discuss in the subsequent chapters) flexibly and adaptively distinguishes his vision from many other ancient economic thinkers. At a conceptual level, Kautilya's economic concepts predated many of the contemporary economic thinkers, which makes him, in my opinion, the most pre-eminent economist in history. While I won't get into the details of the historical comparisons in this book, Table 2.3 summarises them for readers. It clearly shows the genesis of concepts such as opportunity cost, demand-supply frameworks, moral hazard, consumer and producer surplus, asymmetric information in the *Arthashastra* and its re-emergence in more recent centuries by other thinkers.

TABLE 2.3 : *Genesis of Economic Concepts Used by Kautilya*

Genesis of concepts in the Arthashastra *during 4th century* BCE	*Re-emergence of these concepts*	
	Author	Year
Opportunity Cost	Wieser	1889
Demand-Supply Framework	Marshall	1870
Diminishing Returns	Turgot	1766
Liquidity	Keynes	1936
'All other things being equal'	D Bernoulli	1738
Marginal Analysis	Turgot	1766
Constrained Optimization	Walras, Sultsky	1874-1877, 1915
Distinction between Short Run and Long Run	Marshall	1870
Moral Hazard	Adam Smith	1776
Linear Income Tax	Mirrlees	1971
Pubic Goods	Lindahl, Samuelson	1919, 1954

Genesis of concepts in the Arthashastra *during 4th century BCE*	*Re-emergence of these concepts*	
Producer Surplus	Marshall	1870
Importance of Capital Formation	Adam Smith	1776
Theory of Gains from Trade	Ricardo	1817
Crime and Punishment	Becker	1968
Efficiency Wages	Marx, Solow	1867, 1979
Risk-return Trade-off	Markowitz	1952
Asymmetric Information	Akerlof	1970
Time Inconsistency Problem	Kyland-Presscott	1977
Non-cooperative Game	Waldegrave, Nash	1713, 1951
Contingency Planning	H Stein	1996

Source: Sihag 2014

CHALLENGES IN TRANSLATING THE *ARTHASHASTRA*—THE IMPORTANCE OF TANTRAYUKTI[2]

I have mentioned the challenges that surround translating the *Arthashastra* several times in this book. While this might sound repetitive, its importance and neglect by scholars make me reiterate its importance.

There are three broad implications of these challenges which are detailed in this section. First, the

[2] This section is lead authored by Dr S. Sushrutha (assistant professor, teaching Samskritam at Amritha Vishwa Vidyapeetham) and Sriram Balasubramanian.

interpretations of the current translations need to be viewed in a particular context and interpreted based on that context. Second, it would also imply that some of the techniques used for translations, despite the best intentions, are not adequate. We could get more refined perspectives based on the techniques used in the next section.

Lastly, it helps to instil humility in the reader. Sometimes, our modern educated minds tend to pre-suppose that our way of thinking and knowledge structures are better than everything that came before us. These techniques challenge this notion and reiterate that ancient minds had their own techniques and approaches which weren't always inferior to modern ones. It also further reinforces that exploration of the *Arthashastra* through such techniques is an ongoing process that can provide us new insights as we dwell deeper. Understandably, readers who are not familiar with linguistics might find this section dense, but the dilution of its core will take its essence away.

The challenges faced by the authors while translating a work from one language to the other, especially Samskrutha granthas, need to be made explicit for the sake of a reader to be objective. It is not very challenging for an Indian translator to translate a work into regional languages because the cultural connotation is already established in an author and the audience, whereas a foreign translator must dive deep into the cultural aspects of this land to see through the authors' intent.

Initially, every central or peripheral field of literature in ancient India was envisioned to reveal the nuanced and esoteric ideas hidden in the Vedas depending upon the audience of the time. Be it Vedanga, *Upaveda*, *Upanga* and later developments in the lineage of composing technical works such as *Natyashastra*, *Shilpashastra*, *Rasashastra*, among others, had the only goal of unearthing the inner meaning of the Vedas. However, the Veda-centric approach slowly switched to peripheral goals, forgetting the original idea. An important aspect to consider when evaluating a translated work is the extent to which it intimately represents Vedic thought. Ultimately, all works should uplift the reader from the present status of unhappiness to the highest state of bliss.

The Vedangas, limbs of the Vedas, protect them by exploring the systematic approach inherently embedded in the Vedic system of knowledge while focusing on the following aspects—shiksha (शिक्षा), the correctness of pronunciation of mantras to maintain the original way it was revealed to a rishi; vyakarana (व्याकरणम्), grammatical aspects of establishing the legitimate usage and the origin of a word; chandas (छन्दः), the rhythmic arrangements of mantras belonging to each Veda; nirukta (निरुक्तम्), an etymological analysis with a thesaurus of words in the Vedas; jyothishya (ज्योतिषम्), a science of fixing the right time to perform all sorts of actions especially Vedic yajnas (यज्ञः); and kalpa (कल्पः), a procedural exploration into the methodology of performing yajnas.

In the context of understanding and interpreting the Vedas, one must be proficient in the above-mentioned areas of study. To become proficient in these areas requires at least a decade of culturally rooted training—so often lacking in non-indigenous scholars. A yardstick for any translator, especially of the Vedas, is the expertise one has in Vedangas. The biggest challenge for the contemporary generation motivated to obtain

Vedic knowledge is the lack of choice in selecting an authentic translator.

Coming to the field of peripheral knowledge areas, compared to the Vedas such as Ayurveda, the *Arthashastra*, *Dharma Shastra* and so on also require a special set of skills to identify the mind of an author, but does not require the complete knowledge of all the Vedangas. Thought models such as mimamsa, vyakarana, nyaya among others will be crucial study areas for translation and interpretation work. In this context, Ayurveda and the *Arthashastra* have a unique system called Tantrayuktis to not deviate from the central theme of the work.

In subsequent paragraphs, we first deal with the challenges faced by a translator and how through the use of simple techniques they can be addressed.

It not only helps the interpreters or translators but also the reader to ensure they can identify misinterpretations and stick to the original ideas.

KEY PARAMETERS IN THE STRUCTURE OF ANCIENT TEXTS

Field of Knowledge/Primary Focus

Siddhanta (सिद्धान्तः, proponent) or Purvapaksha (पूर्वपक्षः, opponent): A concretised idea to be presented as a substantial work should be based on some axioms that when framed into a philosophical doctrine creates a narrative unity in the rest of the work. One needs to be unambiguous about the central proposition around which the entire narration is built. Sarvadarshanasangraha

(सर्वदर्शनसङ्ग्रहः) of Sayanamadhava stands as an example of original Shastric discourse where every method is implemented. Starting from Charvaka (चार्वाकः) and ending with Shankara Darshana, it is a classic example of how to propose an idea, register the merits and demerits of an argument and finally conclude the series of arguments logically in terms of experiential wisdom is the format of *Sarvadarshanasangraha*, which generally is followed in every Shastra. This one identification of a central theme clarifies many doubts thus discarding misinterpretation or references made out of context.

Sambandha Pariksha is a classic example of a work that presents an opponent's idea to nyaya sambandhas (relations detailed in *Nyaya Shastra*). It analyses the nature of relations between the matter and things beyond the matter as well proposed by *Nyaya Shastra* and tries to explain the intricacies of relationships. Any concept or thought in *Sambandha Pariksha* is in opposition to nyaya in totality. Therefore, one cannot misquote a statement from the whole book.

In this context, one needs to identify whether a work is siddhanta (proponent) or an opponent to the other work which determines the stand.

Audience

Every Shastra has four factors in it to establish an internal consistency: adhikari (अधिकारी: qualified seeker), vishaya (विषयः subject matter of the book), sambandha (सम्बन्धः mutual relation between the subject, seeker, and outcome) and prayojana (प्रयोजनम्: purpose or result). The very structure of these four factors determines the audience with a specific goal of authoring a book.

Not all books are written for everyone. Along with inquisitiveness on a subject, one must be equipped with the necessary tools, including language, clarity of thought and so on, in specified fields of knowledge. For instance, to be an entrepreneur one must be aware of the present market trends and dynamics of modern economic advancements. One needs to be intelligent enough to understand the investment strategies and have an innate passion to succeed to do well in the business world. Similarly, to read Vedantic texts, a seeker's mind must be pure (chittashuddhi, चित्तशुद्धिः) to truly understand the crux of Vedantic teachings.

Always, an important factor is the audience for whom a piece of work has been written. Puranas (पुराणम्) and Ithihasas (इतिहासः) address the day-to-day issues of a common man; therefore, they have intense emotion and belief, stronger than harsh, robust logic to inculcate values and principles of life. Glorification of characters, an aesthetic presentation of divine entities and a dynastical chronology of events of great kings, rishis and yogis are the methods used by Ithihasas and Puranas.

Darshanas (दर्शनम्) are meant for people who are philosophically logical and question everything confronted, nothing accepted without questioning. Dissecting the true nature of the world, debating in a scholarly manner for sharpening the mind, thought experiments, life experiments and exploring the inner world are the methods used in Darshanas and Smritis (स्मृतिः) to assess the situation objectively to come to a definite conclusion. The Vedas (वेदाः Samhita संहिता, Brahmana ब्राह्मणम्, Aranyaka आरण्यकम्, and Upanishads उपनिषत्) are the sources of deepest knowledge that address the minority of individuals who need just one push to experience the reality by shravana, manana and nididdhyasana.

Often, the majority falls prey to Vedantic teachings as it offers a feel-good effect. Rather than making itself qualified by further purifying the mind, this majority starts interpreting the Vedas with unequipped intellect and fails to guide other people on the right path. One of the mantras of the *Kathopanishad* says that, to a qualified one, wisdom (ज्ञानम्) opens itself up completely. Keeping all this in mind, for a layperson to understand and interpret the Vedas is not advisable. That's the very reason the next versions of the same knowledge of the Vedas, and its principles, are further simplified and made user-friendly for the layperson in the form of Itihasa and Purana, Kavya, Darshans, Upavedas, Shastras and Sahitya etc.

The *Arthashastra* (the wisdom of managing knowledge, human resource, wealth and so on for human transformation) is an important work to be studied by every student of management, irrespective of their field of specialisation. The framework of the *Arthashastra* provides a structure of social and cultural ethos completely derived from Vedic origins. A notable feature of every Indian shastrakara (author of a Shastra) is the humble submission of accepting their work to be either sourced from or inspired by Vedic literature, and the authors' contribution is only in compiling or explaining invisible, nuanced ideas to a budding mind in that specific field. The Indian management system is heavily dependent on the principles of the *Arthashastra*, be it from Kautilya, Shukra or Vidura, ultimately referring to the Vedic worldview.

Interpreting the *Arthashastra* that is inclined towards a Vedic worldview is undoubtedly a challenging task for non-indigenous thinkers. Therefore, a tailor-made set of tools, Tantrayuktis (तन्त्रयुक्तिः), is devised specially to anchor the whole narrative and discourse in Vedic ideology, added as an annexure, the last chapter (15th Adhyaya) where a reader gets clarity on the line of thought, which will be explained later in this chapter.

The complexity of the work, the level of language difficulty, logical flow and so on will be a matter of concern and highly dependent on the type of reader. Perhaps, the aspect of adhikara (अधिकारः, qualification) clarifies the ambiguity to a large extent regarding who should study what and what not, how and how not, and why and why not.

Historical Consideration

Many Dharma Shastras and Smritis (a compilation of accepted and summarised social norms and value-based judiciary), such as Yajnavalkya, Manu, Parashara smirits have two sections in general—time-bound rules and time-independent values for humanity. It is important to distinguish between the two sections for a more balanced and objective view of the text.

Basic and Technical Grammar

The knowledge of root and suffix combination to construct a meaningful usable word (prakriti-pratyaya-vivek प्रकृति-प्रत्यय-विवेकः) plays a major role in the Samskritam language, which is an essential pre-requisite. Along with knowledge of grammar, the basic foundation in logic is also required. काणादं पाणिनीयं च सर्वशास्त्रोपकारकम् ('logic and grammar are very essential areas of study for beginning any Shastra') is a popular quote on the importance of vyakarana.

The purpose of the existence of vyakarana is to establish the sadhutva (साधुत्वम्, legitimacy) of all words originating from the minds of rishis or apta (an accepted figure in a society in terms of Vedic wisdom, self-experience and spiritual aspiration). For centuries, Panini's grammar stood as the most accepted version, despite significant contributions from earlier grammarians'. The following section deals with the most critical grammatical rules to be kept in mind while reading a Shastra. In fact, every little detail of vyakarana is important, but because of its wide range of applications, one needs to limit the scope of knowledge of grammar for the sake of understanding a text without being a grammarian.

GENERAL AND ETYMOLOGICAL CONSTRUCT OF LANGUAGE

Any language comprises broadly two levels of understanding—general and etymological. In Samskritam, these are called rudhyartha (the popular meaning of a word), which is part of sambhashana Samskritam (spoken Samskritam), and yaugikartha (the technical meaning with etymological and contextual meaning, which appears especially in various shastras). Therefore, a translator or an interpreter of a shastra must be a serious student of foundational grammar with its popular usage and technical grammar focusing on etymological and contextual usage. There is nothing much to discuss in the spoken language but there is a lot to explore when it comes to technical grammar.

Every word in Samskritam, subject, verb, predicate and so on, are called padam, which, in a usable form, is divided into three sections: subanta (सुबन्तः, the word form suffixed to 'sup' [सुप], generally nouns), tinanta (तिङन्तः, the word form suffixed to 'tin' [तिङ्], verbs, mostly indicator of action) and avyaya (आव्ययः, non-origin of root—suffix or prefix do not matter).

Dhaatu (धातुः) refers to the root of a word as listed by Panini and other rishis. A dhaatu may have innumerable meanings with different shades and modes. Depending on the context, different meanings may be considered as intended by the speaker or the author for which tatparya-lingas have to be referred. For example, gamlr (गम्लृ) is a dhaatu that means movement in general. All the dhaatus having the meaning of 'movement' also equally mean 'learning' in a different context when a speaker intends it. Therefore, just because it is popularly meant in a certain way may not necessarily have the same meaning in the Shastras. Technically, this intended meaning by a speaker is called saamarthya in Samskritam. A wide range of information on the multiplicity of the meaning of one dhaatu facilitates the correct interpretation of the text.

Special Usage with Etymological Specifics

Pratyaya (प्रत्ययः): If there is a dhaatu with multiple meanings as revealed by rishis, it requires a set of suffixes (pratyayas) such as krit, taddhit and so on to exhibit its meaning. A mere dhaatu is not a usable form. Interestingly, all the pratyayas also add on their meanings along with the dhaatu's meaning, which makes them more complex to work with; it's the multiplication of meanings of the dhaatu and pratyaya. In each usage of the word, it has growing permutations, and figuring out the intent becomes complex. In some cases, a pratyaya is used not with the prominent meaning it is assigned to but to the meaning it indirectly signifies. For example, the objective case (dvitiya vibhakti) indicates the object in a sentence, but the locative case (saptami vibhakti) is also used to indicate the object. Therefore, for clarity, a reader must know which pratyayas are exhibiting which meaning of the dhaatu in which context.

Karaka (कारकम्): Once the word is formed in a usable manner in consent with the dhaatu and pratyaya, its placement in a sentence formation depends on the role that the speaker wants to attach to that entity. For example, Kautilya says, 'प्रथमे रात्रिभागे गूढपुरुषान् पश्येत्' (01.19.18), which means 'in the first portion of the night, the king should meet spies'. In this statement, 'meeting' is an action that is the primary anchoring factor. If the question is asked who meets, then the king comes into the picture. When it is about whom the king should meet, then spies have the role and when should he meet them, then the time specification becomes relevant. This is how even the anvaya paddhati (a sequential organisation of the words from verses of Samskritam) works—focusing on an action of the statement and connecting the rest of the components with it. Each component that has a connection with the action will be called karaka. There are six karakas, and there are seven vibhaktis (cases) to indicate the karakas.

Upasarga (उपसर्गः): Along with pratyaya, there are upasargas (prefixes), when added to a word, help to make the sentence more logical. Upasargas have many functions. They may retain the same meaning of dhaatu, produce the opposite meaning, increase the impact of the meaning of dhaatu and so on. The most popular example is as follows: prahaara (pra+haara, प्रहारः) which means hitting, ahaara (aa+haara, आहारः) which means food, ummar (vi+haara, विहारः) which means rejoicing, samhaara (sam+haara, संहारः) which means killing and parihaara (pari+haara, परिहारः) which means a solution. All these multiple meanings are not visible without the prefixes but exist in dhaatu. Therefore, understanding these upasargas is also very important.

Shabda-bodha-prakriya (शाब्दबोधप्रक्रिया): This is the process of comprehending the meaning of speech. The ultimate purpose of any communication is to understand the meaning of speech. Both, vyakarana (व्याकरण, word analysis) and mimamsa (मीमांसा, method of summarising the intent), work hand in hand when it comes to comprehending what is spoken or written. While vyakarana enforces the fundamental tool, speech, to be as close as possible to the mind of a speaker, mimamsa provides a framework through which the intended meaning is comprehended by a listener. Mutually, both try to interpret whose opinion is correct in terms of providing word analysis and summarizing the intent. Surprisingly, both contribute to the same cause from the speakers' and listeners' viewpoints.

Taking consensus from all the inputs given by shastrakaras, Ayurveda and the *Arthashastra* devised a set of tools to incorporate very critical points such as grammar, context, audience and so on for a clear-cut interpretation without any room for misunderstanding.

A NOTE ON TANTRAYUKTI

It's quite difficult to identify the intention of an author unless one is immersed in their mind. A translator or an interpreter must be familiar with the culture, ideology and inner dynamics of a tradition in order to comprehensively understand its texts. This is the challenge that we are facing today at the global level where anthropology plays an important role, especially in academia. The Vedic tradition has not been explored enough to make it as relevant as it could be for the same reason stated above. Shastras (technical work) such as Veda, Dharma, Artha, Kama, Moksha, Nyaya, Tarka, Tantra, Yoga, Agama, Smriti, Itihasa, among others either have not been understood, partially understood or completely misunderstood, giving rise to misinterpretations for the simple reason that such translators have not dived into the mind of an author or purposefully mislead the reader.

To make the intention of an author explicit, an internal mechanism has been identified in every Shastra pertaining to its method of delivering discourse. This intention is called taatparya (तात्पर्यम्, intent). The determination of taatparya in Vedanta happens based on six lingas (taatparya linga, logical indicators):

उपक्रमोपसंहारौ अभ्यासोऽपूर्वता फलम्।
अर्थवादोपपत्ती च लिङ्गं तात्पर्यनिर्णये॥

Upakrama-upasaṃhaara (उपक्रमोपसंहारौ) means introduction and conclusion. In the *Bhagavad Gita*, Sri Krishna says that all of Arjuna's problems originated from shoka and moha in the beginning and ended when moha and shoka are discarded and memory is gained.

Abhaaysa (अभ्यासः) means repetition. Sri Krishna keeps repeating the nature of atma in the second, thirteenth, fifteenth and other chapters to keep Arjuna focused on atmatattva.

Apurvata (अपूर्वताः) is originality. To a specific audience, whatever method Krishnadvaipayana followed to convey the pragmatic solutions for social conflicts at the time of the Mahabharata was a unique way of presenting the Vedic teaching.

Phala (फलम्) is the result. With what result the discourse is being expounded determines the focus of the text. Sri Krishna intends to dispel the confusion and grief of Arjuna.

Arthavada (अर्थवादः) is a motivational word. When Arjuna says that he is ready to fight and beg for alms, Sri Krishna motivates him to fight by introducing promotional ideas such as svarga, naraka, keerti, bhaya, etc.

Upapatti (उपपत्तिः) is substantiation. Arjuna's mind was covered by infatuation with ahimsa for which Sri Krishna had to logically correct him with all the substantial nature of atma that does not have birth and death and so on.

This is how Vedanta makes conceptual intention explicit by implementing either one or a combination of more indicators (taatparya linga, तात्पर्यलिङ्गम्) to determine the intent of an author. The context and intent in Vedanta are relatively simple when compared to complex shastras such as Ayurveda, Smriti and the *Arthashastra*. For these, the interpreter needs a finely structured system to understand, present, debate and deliberate logically to get to the root of the intent.

In the word Tantrayuktis (तन्त्रयुक्तिः), tantra means identified shastra and yukti means assembling and compiling. The methodology of composing and interpreting any shastra came into the picture to address the issues of comprehending, ideating, structuring, interpreting and creating a shastra, especially the *Arthashastra* and Ayurveda. These two works have Tantrayuktis at the end of the works.

The number of Tantrayuktis differs from shastra to shastra according to the subject matter and the field of knowledge with which it is connected. In Ayurveda, for Sushrutha it's thirty-six, for Charaka it's thirty-two and in Chanakya's *Arthashastra*, the number of Tantrayuktis is also thirty-two. Some definitions of a yukti with the same name from the shastras also differ in relation to the context and situation.

The *Sushrutha Samhita* identifies two main functions of Tantrayuktis; vakya yojanam (वाक्ययोजनम्), which is integrating the unconnected sentences and artha yojanam (अर्थयोजनम्), which is integrating the invisible and unrelated conceptual meanings. Further, Sushrutha elaborates in the next two shlokas that these Tantrayuktis invalidate the incorrect stand of an opponent and validate the accurate meaning from one's viewpoint. Tantrayuktis also make clear the following factors in its methodology;

visible but explicitly unexpressed, clearly not made explicit, partially told but unclear, will be clarified while discoursing the content along with suitable examples.

However, the principles of Tantrayuktis may be traced back to Purva-Mimamsa as it contributes to extracting the exact meaning from the Vedas. It rules out the possibility of a wrong conclusion.

We will ponder upon some of the Tantrayuktis for the benefit of the reader as to how it helps a reader not to deviate from the focus of discourse of any particular shastra.

Kautilya's (Chanakya) thirty-two Tantrayuktis are not given in detail below. We have tried to elaborate on some selected ones to make them understandable for the reader.

Adhikarana (अधिकरणम्) is the main topic of discussion and discourse to which the section of a book or the book itself is dedicated.

Probably all the earlier works on artha, dealing with the acquisition and maintaining the value of wealth such as land, money and so on, and using for the purpose stated in the shastras, have been summarised in the *Arthashastra*, which will be the course of discussion of this text.

In the *Arthashastra*, the focus is on the topic 'artha', the means of experiencing pleasure and bliss. Anything which will be discussed here has to be artha. One cannot expect the nature of reality (atma-svarupa, आत्मस्वरूपम्) and argue about atma simply because that is not the subject matter of the *Arthashastra*. Within the *Arthashastra*, one may find sub-sections of a chapter dealing with taxation rules for the citizens; taxation rules are the 'adhikarana' until a new topic is started.

One cannot expect lessons on technical details of quantum theory in a biology classroom or optical imaging in a philosophy class. Whichever topic is clearly stated, that is the adhikarana of that section or the whole text itself.

Here, the Adhikarana Yukti clarifies what to expect and what not to from a selected section of the work.

Vidhaana (विधानम्) is stating the sequence of topics or the actions to be dealt with. Kautilya, in the first chapter, just lists out the topics he is going to elaborate on in a particular sequence; knowledge source, association with elders, control over the senses and so forth, in a logical sequential manner. This advocacy of sequence itself is 'vidhanam'. The reason behind following a particular sequence is very logical. In the beginning, he establishes the necessity of the *Arthashastra*, then its navigation within the Vedic knowledge source, then comes down to the level of the contemporary situation of wealth, money, economics, human resources and so on in a certain way of thinking and presenting that would draw an audience to dive deep into the subject.

Modern scientific research articles follow a specific sequence of presentation; background, aims and objectives, literature survey, materials and methods, data presentation, discussion and conclusion. The aim and objectives of the research should be quoted in the beginning, not at the end. Likewise, research will not be concluded at the beginning of a research article, but at the end.

Similarly, Tantrayukti advocates a sequential discourse of different topics at various levels, eradicating illogical presentation. All shastras have an inherent logic based on the axioms portrayed by the shastra and have been built systematically to convey the message to an identified audience. There are thirty-two such Tantrayuktis that need to be taken into consideration for a reasonable analysis of the *Arthashastra*. No doubt that some scholars would have taken the effort to do this but every analysis doesn't necessarily include this crucial component. Unless these are incorporated, the authentic meanings of the *Arthashastra* will remain subdued.

In retrospect, what did we deal with in this section? We looked at the four key parameters for interpreting ancient texts: field of knowledge, audience, historical context, and basic grammar. While these broad contours serve as a guide, the foundations are laid in the grammar and etymology which we had illustrated through the basics of Samskritam. Following the etymology, we focus on the concept of Tantrayukti and its relevance to the *Arthashastra*. Not only do these highlight the amount of research needed to understand the *Arthashastra*, but it also showcases the multi-dimensionality of the subject at hand.

The contemporary mind through its modern intellectual framework isn't always going to grasp this holistically without the anubhava (अनुभवः) of immersing oneself into the cultural fabric of the text at hand. Besides highlighting the complexity (which is often ignored by others), it also presents an opportunity to give our humble salutations to the multi-dimensionality of the text before we move ahead in the book.

3

Economic and Philosophical Frameworks—Dharmic Capitalism

ECONOMIC FRAMEWORK (अर्थ-अन्वीक्षिकी)—LAISSEZ-FAIRE, KEYNESIAN OR DHARMIC CAPITALISM?

Modern economic thinkers provide a binary distinction between economic paradigms—either the laissez-faire approach or the Keynesian interventionist approach to policymaking.

Laissez-faire is broadly defined as 'a doctrine opposing governmental interference in economic affairs beyond the minimum necessary for the maintenance of peace and property rights'.[1] Its proponents believe that government intervention should be at a bare minimum and that the markets should determine the functioning of the economy. The Keynesian approach on the other hand is broadly defined as one where 'optimal economic performance could be achieved—and economic slumps prevented—by influencing aggregate demand through activist stabilisation and economic intervention policies by the government'.[2] In simpler terms, they advocate

[1] https//www.merriam-webster.com/dictionary/laissez-faire

[2] https//www.investopedia.com/terms/k/keynesianeconomics.asp

that the state should intervene when the market is not functioning properly and that this intervention is necessary for the economy to do well.

In my view, Kautilyan thinking is somewhere in between these two economic paradigms with the distinction of being underpinned by the foundation of dharma. Some researchers argue that Kautilyan thinking is akin to a state-controlled economy, something similar to the erstwhile Soviet Union-style planning commissions. As we will see later in this chapter and the rest of the book, this is far from the case.

I tend to agree, to a large extent, with other scholars, who have defined Kautilya's governance through four main components: varta (economic policy), dandaneeti (law and enforcement), anvikshiki (philosophical and ethical framework) and trayi (cultural context). These are well-thought-out and valid interpretations of the Kautilyan approach and provide other researchers with a foundation to explore further.

Having said that, I tend to disagree on a few counts from this approach. First, I find trayi to be a common feature across the various pillars rather than a separate pillar by itself. I try to highlight these cultural elements in the various pillars of dharmic capitalism later in the chapter. Second, and most importantly, the idea of dharma as a foundational principle was essential to his economic worldview. Without the philosophy of dharma, Kautilya's economic principles are a skyscraper without a foundation. This must be the most important component of any Kautilyan economic framework. I define this detailed framework as dharmic capitalism.

Dharmic Capitalism

There are three pillars to Kautilyan dharmic capitalism: A rule-based yet non-intrusive state, wealth creation through a global outlook and the need for sustainable growth and welfare.

FIGURE 3.1: *Components of Dharmic Capitalism*

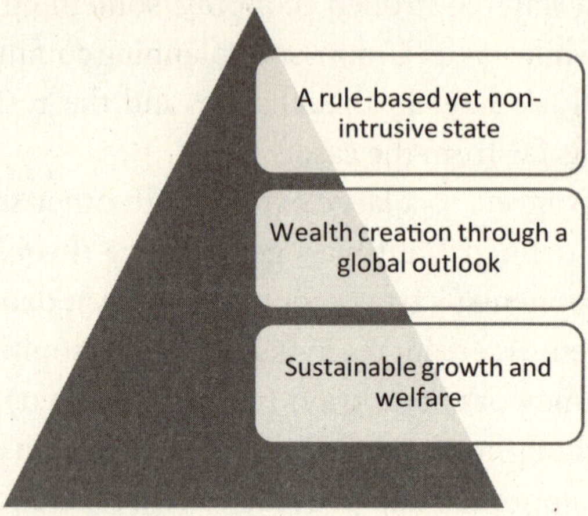

Rule-based Yet Non-intrusive State

The role of the state, as conceptualised by Kautilya, is one that is firm and rule-based yet not intrusive in its implementation. The plethora of rules and regulations for various industries indicates a rule-based framework for governance as opposed to an excessively planned economy. For example, let's take trade policy for instance. As we detail later in the book, Kautilya wanted fixed duties and tariffs for products and exempted some of these for imports to boost trade between the borders of different kingdoms. While the basic tenets are strictly followed, there is no 'executive planning' of sorts in its execution. There seems to be no limit on the productive capacities of firms pertaining to what they produce and how they produce. The focus seems to be mainly on having a robust regulatory and legal framework that is strictly implemented. Otherwise, the nitty-gritty of the processes is flexible enough to ensure that they function properly and as per consumer interests. The focus of all of Kautilya's thinking on implementation is on the consumer's best interests, which is contrarian to the role of what is called a 'planned economy' in modern parlance.

Does this mean that the state is not interventionist at all? Not really. Kautilya seems to feel the need to intervene when the market is not able to sort out certain things. For example, as we detail in the 'Sustainable Growth and Welfare' chapter, Kautilya feels strongly about the need for matsya nyaya, which means ensuring that small firms do not get overwhelmed by bigger or dominant firms. In this particular case, he feels the need to intervene so that the richer firms/people pay their fair share of income so that inequalities are not exacerbated. This is an instance where he feels the state needs to 'nudge' the policy in a way that ensures parity to the people in the kingdom.

Wealth Creation Through a Global Outlook

At a macro level, Kautilya seems to be inclined towards a global view of the economy. This has three components: a vibrant international trade environment through ease of doing business, utilising natural resources and traits of the populace, and enabling investment from savings to drive growth in a variety of areas, including infrastructure.

International trade was integral to the functioning of the Mauryan dynasty and the free exchange of knowledge and trade seems to be ingrained in his approach. While he is cognisant of the need to protect domestic interests as well, his policies seem to indicate an expansionist view of the economy. For example, his exemptions and incentives for imports and the efforts taken to make 'ease of doing business' a reality in the kingdom indicate his worldview on this topic.

Furthermore, the emphasis on creating a friendly business environment is self-evident with his focus on streamlining tax measures for all the products being traded.

Infrastructure development through highways, roadways and maritime routes further reiterates that he viewed trade as more of a boon to his kingdom than anything else. It is important to note that the key highways such as the Uttarapath and Dakshnipath (discussed later in the 'Wealth Creation' chapter) were improved and strengthened significantly during the Mauryan rule. Kautilya felt the need to enhance the trade infrastructure to enable better commerce among trading partners. In summary, he felt the need to create wealth through an internationalist mindset and approach.

Sustainable Growth and Welfare

Kautilya also believed that the creation of wealth and its subsequent economic growth had to be sustainable and needed to incorporate the welfare of people. This included components such as environmental sustainability and dealing with inequality in society. He was aware of the challenges of unfettered growth, which could harm the environment and cause inequality in society. There have been references in the *Arthashastra* that emphasise the role of matsya nyaya, which indirectly implies the need for redistribution in policymaking to ensure that the rich don't dominate the poor. Moreover, the discussion of contemporary ideas such as minimum wage indicates his emphasis on protecting the needy and vulnerable as much as possible. He also reiterates that the 'welfare of the people' is the supreme goal of a king or a government.

Like many other processes and systems, there is always a philosophical framework that inspires individuals to develop processes and systems. Kautilya and his dharmic capitalism are no different. So, what is the philosophical framework underpinning it? In my view, the philosophy of dharma and its tripartite foundational dharmic elements of ethics, responsibilities and harmonious well-being are central to the philosophical framework that inspired dharmic capitalism.

Dharma and its Role in Prosperity

The foundational elements of Kautilya's economic policy revolve around the role of dharma[3] in economic policymaking. The definition of dharma is

[3] The definition of dharma has both a spiritual and social component. For the narrow purposes of this book, we stick to its relevance to the role of the state and its economic policy.

multilayered and has many meanings attached to it. It's illustrated beautifully in the following shloka below:

धृतिः क्षमा दमो-अस्तेयं, शौचम् इन्द्रिय-निग्रहः ।
धीः विद्या सत्यम् अक्रोधो दशकं धर्म-लक्षणम् ॥
मनुस्मृतिः 6.92 ॥[4]

dhṛtiḥ kṣamā damo-Asteyaṁ śaucam Indriya-nigrahaḥ |
dhīḥ vidyā satyam Akrodho daśakaṁ dharma-lakṣaṇam ||manusmṛtiḥ 6.92||

In simplified form, the shloka implies that dharma is defined by patience, forgiveness, control over your mind, non-stealing, cleanliness of body, mind and soul, restrain on your senses, proper use of intellect, proper knowledge of God, soul and nature, honesty, and control over your anger.

In this book, for the sake of convenience and the relevance to socio-economic policies, we have simplified these attributes in the context of socio-economic policies into three main categories: ethics, responsibilities and harmony. The following paragraphs discuss these components of dharma and their impact on Kautilya's economic worldview.

Kautilya and Dharma

Kautilya talks about the need for 'Ahimsa, satyam, cleanliness and freedom, compassion and tolerance'

[4] https://theomtemple.org/what-is-dharma-as-per-vedic-teachings/

(Sihag 2017, 107) as foundational to his socio-economic policies. Kautilya believed that one couldn't have sustainable economic prosperity without these foundational elements. It is important to note that he believed in the rule of law but felt that without a strong ethical foundation it was difficult to enforce it on a large scale. His thinking has been largely inspired by the ideals of dharma addressed by thinkers before him. This has also been mentioned by Sihag (2014) in his book.

How is all of this relevant to us?

One of the pillars of any developed country in the modern world has been ethics, which refers to honest and corruption-free society. If there is one thing that would be transformative in India's rise, it is the elimination of corruption. Bribery has been ingrained into the ecosystem; be it the cop on the street wanting money to overlook a traffic violation, the traffic inspector who wants it for getting a driving license or the casual corruption that takes place while buying properties are a few examples. Every public activity for Indians is rife with multiple instances of corruption by public officials.

Responsibility is another central pillar in society. Be it towards the family or society, there is an inherent social contract that we view through the lens of responsibility. For example, how many times have we heard of family members supporting others financially without expecting anything in return? If individuals are responsible for their kith and kin and take care of them, then at an aggregate the economic system becomes more sustainable.

Harmonious living with compassion and tolerance is very important for a peaceful society. One of India's most beautiful tenets is how people from various religions and cultures come together and live peacefully. Without a peaceful society, no economic machine can move forward and ensure a country's prosperity. Moreover, our day-to-day well-being is also enhanced when we live in peace and harmony with society. In the bigger picture, these things are central to any society's progress and serve as foundations of economic prosperity.

FIGURE 3.2: *Components of Dharma That Serve as a Foundation to Kautilyan Economic Thinking*

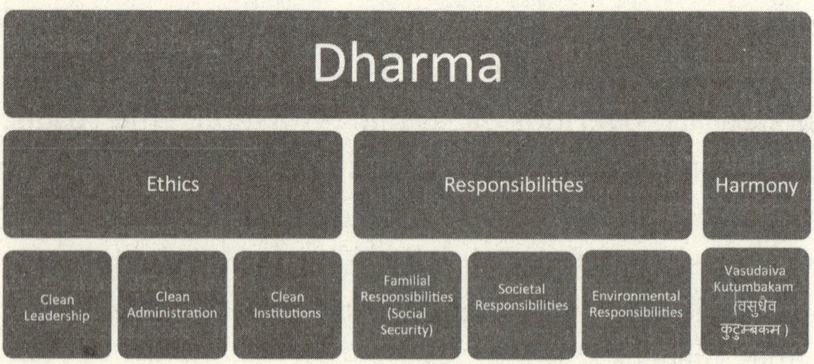

Figure 3.2 provides an overview of the three components of dharma that we deal with in this book. Ethics is segregated into clean leadership, administration and institutions. Responsibilities are classified into familial, societal and environmental while social harmony is viewed through the lens of 'vasudaiva kutumbakam' (the world is one family).

Ethics as a Base to Eradicate Corruption

Numerous studies have indicated that if India were to irradicate corruption, it could improve its GDP by a substantial margin (Obamuyi and Olayiwola 2019). Everyone knows this and they are tired of hearing it; rather, they would like to know how to address this.

Clean leadership

Kautilya emphasised the importance of honesty in the rulers of the land since that serves as a benchmark for the rest of the people. He had suggested that an ethical foundation is the most important quality in a king and education serves as an important tool to achieve his objective. He says, 'Just as a clean object is stained with whatever is smeared on it so a prince with a fresh mind understands as the truth whatever is taught to him. Therefore, a prince should be taught what is dharma and artha, not what is unrighteous and materially harmful (1.17).' These ideals are very much applicable to some of the current challenges in addressing corruption in India.

Clean administration

The repeated emphasis by Kautilya in the *Arthashastra* on upholding Raj dharma serves as an important reminder of the need for a clean administration. In that light, he firmly believed in accountability within the administration and amongst the kith and kin of the ruler. There are specific instances where he focuses on the need for transparency at an institutional level—something akin to the modern-day Right to Information (RTI) Act, which serves as a transparency tool to keep the public servants in check. Some measures proposed include highlighting the revenues generated by the fines and gifts from public servants and sharing the expenditure details of the palace so that everyone else below it is forced to disclose their accounts for public scrutiny (Sihag 2014).

Clean institutions

The role of good governance and institution-building wasn't just seen through the ethical lens but also through the prism of being a determinant of growth and ensuring better returns on private investment. Kautilya believed that by reducing corruption in public officials (through government reform) and by removing administrative roadblocks to economic activity, growth will improve significantly as a by-product of this. As highlighted in (Sihag 2014), this also serves to improve the Markowitz–Sharpe efficiency curves with greater return and lesser risk for investment.

Responsibilities as Determinants of Sustainable Growth and Welfare

Most Western worldviews largely focus on freedom and rights-based approaches but less so on responsibilities. However, Indian society is largely responsibility driven, at least on a practical day-to-day level. Not surprisingly, Kautilya viewed responsibilities to be central to this economic philosophy.

Familial responsibilities and social security

Whether it is responsibility towards family or society, it plays an important role in how economic decisions are made. For example, the role of families in the economic ecosystem is largely tailored to how the Indian society functions. It serves as a form of 'social security' for members of a particular family. You may have heard of people providing financial support to other family members without expecting anything in return.

Many businesses in India rely on such informal connections, so much so that such a form of financing is integral to economic activity in the country. Take the example of a *kirana* shop down your street. Most of the financing for the shop is done either through social connections through the family or informal networks among people. There is very little interface with formal financial institutions such as banks for financing these businesses.

While I am not arguing in favour of this being the best form of financing (nor over-romanticising the need for it, as there could be other better forms), the reality is that community-based financing is still the most dominant in Indian society. As such, the dharmic view of responsibilities is an important factor to understand this aspect of society.

Societal responsibilities

In terms of responsibilities towards society, cleanliness and sustainable living are at the forefront. Kautilya's emphasis on cleanliness, appropriated from dharmic ideals, is an important construct for modern Indian economic thinking. There are many instances in the *Arthashastra* where public societal responsibilities are encouraged, and regulations are implemented to that effect. For example, there were fines imposed on people who trespassed and dirtied public roads and infrastructure.

Kautilyan Factometer

There were various types of fines imposed on people who did not follow societal responsibilities. These include (Rangarajan 1992, 344, 403):

1/8th of pana* for making a public road impassable with dirt, water or mud, 54 panas for having freshwater course in close proximity to a neighbour's house, 1/4th panas for throwing dirt on the royal highways, 106 panas for ploughing over paths, water works and forests, 1000 panas for destroying boundary marks between villages to hide encroachment.

Moreover, there was an emphasis on community responsibilities on a broad thematic level as illustrated in the quote below:

> It is desired that no one should behave in a manner likely to cause any harm to the immediate neighbourhoud (3.20.15). To avoid any inconvenience or confrontation, the houses should be constructed in conformity with the demarcated boundaries to be laid with sufficient space between

* A pana is the name of the currency used in the *Arthashastra*. 1 pana is similar to $1, for example.

two houses (3.8.3-5); parking space for quadrupeds, fire place, water storage arrangements, grinding mill or corn thrashing devices etc. should be placed sufficiently away from a neighbouring house (3.8.11): any construction by way of ditch, outsie projecting staircase, ladder, water channel etc. are to be avoided (3.8.21); and for effecting such arrangements house owners, by mutual agreement, may get things done as desired, and should avoid what is undesirable (3.8.18).

Source: Sunil 1998

These tend to indicate an overarching emphasis on societal responsibilities in governance. Kautilya viewed this as pivotal for having a harmonious society which, in turn, would usher in economic prosperity for the people. Cleanliness and societal responsibilities have been areas where modern-day India has lagged.

However, recent developments have helped to make progress on this front. These include the Swachh Bharath initiative, which has transformed public cleanliness in rural areas (Haque 2019). A WHO study mentioned that this resulted in averting more than 3,00,000 deaths from diarrhoea and protein-deficiency malnutrition between 2014 and October 2019. Then there is also a large amount of investment in renewables and solar power to look at alternative energy sources. These new efforts could be stepped up with a focus on the role of a clean environment in policymaking as advocated by Kautilya many centuries ago.

Environmental responsibilities

Kautilya emphasised the need to protect the environment in various sutras in the *Arthashastra*. These have focused on boosting ecological diversity, protecting natural resources (such as water management) and sustaining the natural environment, among others. All these elements are important components of combating climate change.

In terms of animal biodiversity, there were both responsibilities and legislation to protect animals. For example, the village head ensured that animal cruelty was prevented within his jurisdiction. A slew of jobs was created to monitor this and regulations were put in place by Kautilya to protect the indigenous biodiversity of his kingdom. Kautilya also mentions the need to protect natural resources. His concept of an ideal janapada indicates the need to sustainably protect natural resources for society to grow organically. Much of the sutras discuss the role of preserving resources as a driver of prosperity.

India's environment has been a major source of concern for policymakers, with more than six out of the ten most polluted cities in the world (Broom 2020). The national capital, Delhi, has one of the worst air-quality indices in the world. India is also lagging in the seventeen sustainable development goals (*The Hindu* 2021) that have to be achieved by 2030. Moreover, the large urban environmental mess has created a huge liability for environmental progress in the country. It might be prudent to look at Kautilya's emphasis on the environment and enhance its centrality in policymaking.

Harmonious Living with the World as One Family

Kautilya believed that social harmony was of foremost importance when it came to achieving prosperity in the kingdom (Sihag 2014). Moreover, many ancient texts before the *Arthashastra* have also reiterated the importance of social harmony and well-being through yoga and other ancient practices. Kautilya acknowledges this and reiterates the importance of personal and social harmony and well-being through his text. In a country as multicultural as India, the importance of social harmony can never be underestimated, and it will always remain central to any form of economic progress.

Kautilya firmly believes in the idea of वसुधैव कुटुम्बकम (vasudaiva kutumbakam), which is translated as 'the whole world is one single family'. This is inspired by a famous quote from the *Maha Upanishad*. [6]

Kautilyan Factometer

Mantra VI-72, *Maha Upanishad*

अयं बन्धुरयंनेति गणना लघुचेतसाम्
उदारचरितानां तु वसुधैव कुटुम्बकम ॥ (6.72.42)

It means, 'The distinction, "this person is mine, and this one is not", is made only by the narrow-minded (the ignorant who are in duality). For those of noble conduct (those who know the Supreme Truth), the whole world is one family (one Unit).'

[6] https://resanskrit.com/vasudhaiva-kutumbakam/

Kautilya's thought is inspired by this philosophy of the universe being one family, especially in the context of economic policy ideas. The vast emphasis on trade (detailed in a later chapter) between countries and within the kingdom is a testimony to this sentiment. The emphasis that he gives on improving trade relations with other countries, the preferences given to imports and products, and also the development and usage of various land and maritime routes before and after the Mauryan kingdom further demonstrate the idea of 'one world one family' that the Vedic texts have pronounced for centuries. This is further illustrated by other ideas—especially those related to foreign policy—which he pursued in the *Arthashastra*. There has been research that has highlighted his thinking on foreign policy and the need to navigate international relations to sustain the prosperity of the kingdom.

Cultural and Community Context as a Horizontal across the Pillars

The role of culture and community plays an important underlying horizontal component across all the main pillars mentioned earlier in this section. Kautilya shows on multiple occasions that he isn't comfortable with the one-size-fits-all approach of policy solutions to the economic challenges. For example, his approaches to familial and societal responsibilities reiterate the importance of community involvement in decision-making. There have been other stances where states have different types of economic policies that suit a particular community and its cultural context.

The Dharmic Foundation and Its Economic Relevance

We have discussed the key elements of dharmic capitalism in previous sections. So, what is the big-picture view? Figure 3.3 provides a summary of it.

FIGURE 3.3: *Dharma and Dharmic Capitalism Linkages*

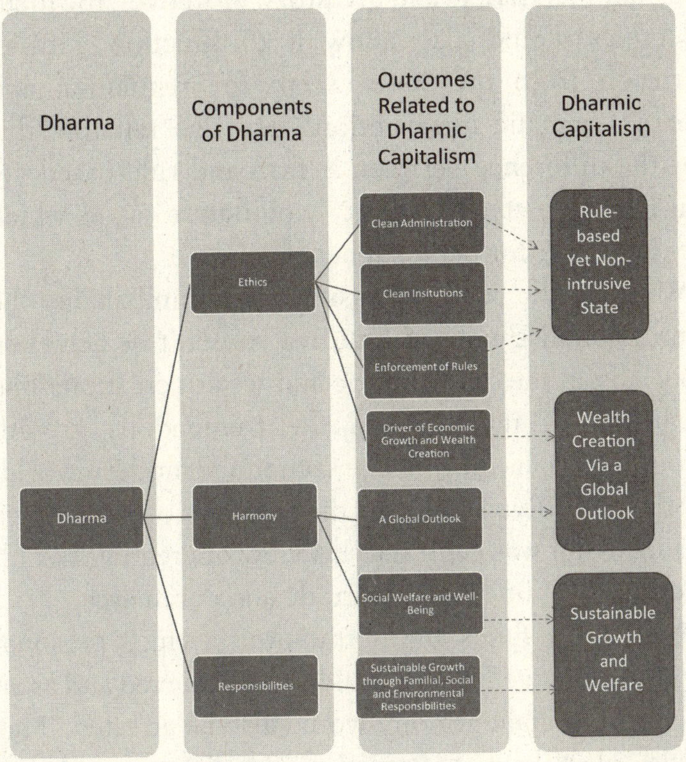

Source: Author's Analysis and creation

Without ethics, Kautilya felt there wouldn't be corruption-free governance in the state, which is central to his idea of a rules-based state. Honesty and corrupt-free practices, according to him, would ensure the people had confidence in the system. This would trickle down to businesses and traders having confidence in the governance structure of the state and the people whom they are dealing with. He thought that this confidence in the system would be important for economic prosperity and as an extension, enhance the internationalist view of the kingdom among international traders and investors. Moreover, the focus on ethics would also allow it to function without intrusion from the state except for regulation and specific thematic interventions. He also felt that this was the difference between a 'firm and rule-based yet non-intrusive state' and an 'exploitative' state which uses its power for personal benefits.

Without the idea of vasudaiva kutumbakam, the internationalist view of Kautilya couldn't be achieved especially in the case of trade and wealth creation. The expansion of markets and the tremendous growth through globalisation can be seen in the modern world. In the Kautilyan world, the theory of vasudaiva kutumbakam was central to his view of creating wealth by optimising international trade and commerce.

Without a focus on harmonious living, personal harmony and well-being couldn't be achieved and as an extension, social harmony would also be affected. This would also lead to social inequalities not being addressed. Hence, the idea of maximising welfare wouldn't be achieved at both the personal and societal levels.

Without responsibilities, he felt that the social fabric would be affected, hence he emphasised its importance in a holistic society. The personal responsibilities would build better cohesion and enable a 'social security' of sorts for individuals, thus providing more incentives for individuals to take risks in business decisions. His advocation of societal responsibilities focused on cleanliness and sustainable living. Furthermore, his focus on environmental responsibilities adds further credence to the need for sustainable living. His views on personal, societal and environmental responsibilities are directly linked to his idea of sustainable growth.

Lastly, the state and the markets serve as a horizontal across the pillars in Figure 3.3. While retaining their individual identities, they are in part derived and anchored to the foundation of dharma and its ideals. Dharma serves as a self-correcting mechanism for both these entities to thrive in a sustainable and balanced manner across time. This ensures that the foundation of capitalism is not on the temporal binary edifice of the market and state but on the eternal dharmic ideals.

In essence, one can see that the economic framework that Kautilya had implemented was largely a derivative of the dharmic ideals which we spoke about earlier. In my view, there seems to be little doubt that Kautilya was pursuing neither laissez-faire nor a Keynesian economic model but dharmic capitalism as highlighted in this section.

4

Wealth Creation

INTERNATIONAL TRADE—THE KAUTILYAN GLOBALISATION TANTRA

International trade has been one of the important pillars of India's economic rise. In simpler terms, trade is defined as the movement of goods and services from one place to another. This can be within countries or between countries. Trade has played an important role in India's post-Independence progress as well as in pre-eminent times.

> **Kautilyan Factometer**
>
> Economic growth is centred on the idea of trade across borders around the world. Kautilya understood this very well. The *Arthashastra* provides various instances of such examples and there is significant evidence to suggest that free trade of goods and services was central to the Kautilyan economic framework.

It's important to note that these distinctions were shared during a time when econometric and statistical methods were nascent and not as comprehensive as they are today. Viewing the ideas in the context of their times would enable the reader to have much greater appreciation of the texts.

History of Trade in India

In Angus Maddison's world-renowned research on global economic history, titled *The World Economy: A Millennial Perspective* (2001), he articulates the importance of trade in India's progress over the centuries. There are many theories about this phenomenal growth with critics suggesting that this was mainly due to the population advantage that India and China had during those times. While this is a possibility, it doesn't align with the anecdotal evidence that we see from travellers and ancient inscriptions. Explorers such as Christopher Columbus, Vasco da Gama, Fei Xin and Marco Polo have all shared their views that India was one of the most prosperous lands in the world for many years. Furthermore, much of the natural resource wealth in the world was in India and China. It is also important to note that in the sectors that were prominent during 0–1750 CE—agriculture, minerals and trade—all had India as one of the world's top producers and consumers of such goods. Many studies have affirmed the importance of trade routes in ancient India, which facilitated the liberal movement of goods and services from various countries into India and vice versa.

Ancient Trade Networks

The ancient trade networks in India consisted of three key elements: the interconnection between various in-land regions, corporate guilds and maritime infrastructure. These three elements were integrated for efficient trade routes. Compared to the modern-day supply-chain infrastructure, it might not have been sophisticated but the conceptual idea of trade infrastructure was in place. The movement of commerce through these routes provided a springboard for various geopolitical manoeuvres from the Mauryan dynasty to the British invasion of India. In that sense, much of the GDP growth and prosperity was a derivative of efficient trade across borders.

Inter-city connectivity

There were thousands of kilometres long trade routes that connected almost all of India through various highways and linkages. The Mahabharata gives instances of various such land routes with references to Uttarpatha (the northern highway linking a variety of northern towns) and Dakshinapatha (the southern highway linking numerous southern cities) which also connected inland commercial centres and the various ports. Ancient trade routes were broadly classified as Mahapatha, Vanikpatha and Rajapatha respectively (Hebalkar 2018).

While the Mahapatha connected the four corners of India through its trading routes, the Vanikpatha were specially designated zones of economic activity. While the national highways were used to connect various corners of India, the Vanikpathas were used as specialised economic zones through which trade was conducted.

They were dominated by caravans (sartha, सार्थ) which carried a wide range of commodities and food source products through the various Vanikpathas in each of the states in each region. Moreover, in Uttarpartha, the trade routes connected the janapadas of each region whereas the Dakshinapatha (southern region) was largely used for connecting inland centres and ports, especially for commodities. These are highlighted in Map 4.1.

MAP 4.1: *Trade Routes in Ancient India*

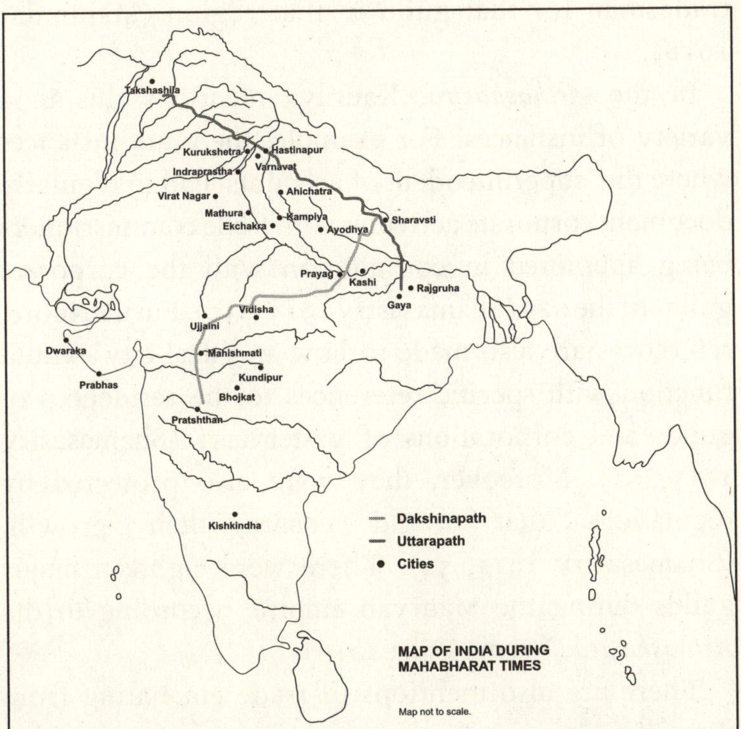

Source: Verma Ojha 2016

Moreover, trade within the Indian subcontinent was common and was often encouraged by rulers as well. There is considerable information to suggest that in many kingdoms, trade played an important role in the overall GDP of those times.

Corporate guilds

The emergence of corporate guilds was a pre-Vedic phenomenon; there were references to the existence of such guilds in *Jathakas*, *Gauthama Dharamasutra* and other ancient scriptures that were estimated to have been written before 800 BCE. The head of these guilds was called a 'sreni' and he was the head tradesman for that guild in that region (Majumdar 1918).

In the *Arthashastra*, Kautilya mentions this in a variety of instances. For example, there are instances where the 'superintendent of accounts' had to regularly document corporate activities with trade commissioners being appointed in consultation with the corporate guilds of the day (Shamasastry 1915, 253). Furthermore, references are also made to how an 'ideal city' would function with specific references to the residences of guilds and corporations of yesteryears (Shamasastry 1915, 61). Moreover, they were also protected by regulations that would ensure their growth. (Shamasastry 1915, 54). There were eighteen major guilds during the Mauryan empire, according to the *Arthashastra* (Verma Ojha 2016).

There are also mentions of trade emanating from the Chola empire in the south to the Suvarnwidpa (Island of Gold or Sumatra) and Yawadpa (Java) through a cluster of ports in Bengal, Odisha, Mahabalipuram and Nagapattinam among others. These ports were one of the most popular ports in southern India between the seventh and ninth centuries during the Pallava dynasty. There were also references to trading and commercial and maritime activities in the region (Sanyal 2013).

They indicate the importance of these guilds and how they served as a network of banks for financing trade (among other business needs) in the country. They were also financed by temples in the region, which, besides their religious purposes, widely served as financing tools for many of these guilds. There is evidence of merchant guilds and temples having contracts signed for trade purposes.

Maritime routes

There have been many anecdotes of Indian maritime history in recent times. The main maritime trade routes in ancient India were the ones along the Erythraean Sea (connecting the western coast of India to the rest of the world) and the Indian Ocean (connecting the southern and eastern parts of India to the rest of South East and East Asia) respectively. These maritime routes provided the 'last-mile delivery' to import and export the goods between major cities in many of these countries.

MAP 4.2: *Maritime Trade Routes in Ancient India*

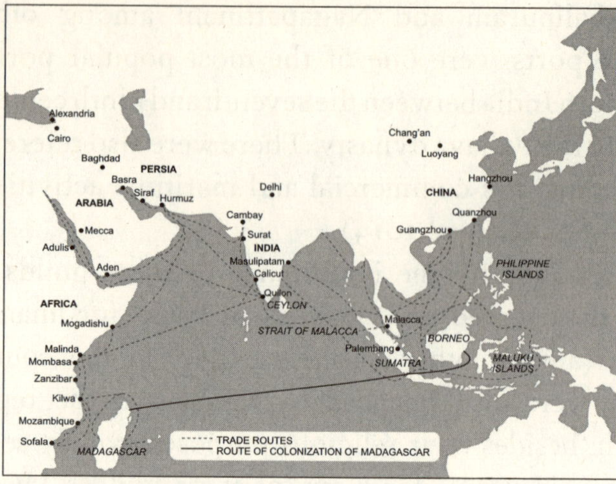

Source: Creative Commons Attribution ShareAlike

Kautilyan references to the department of waterways and ships are very significant as well. There was a 'superintendent for ships' (navadhyaksa), passports, and accounts related to trade (Shamasastry 1915, 131). Some of these roles included details on the monitoring of customs duties on the ports, fishing licenses (naukahatakam) and sailing fees for passengers who came in these ships (yatravetanam) and taxes for individuals living in the coastal areas (kliptam) among others.

All of this seems to indicate that in ancient times, trade was a substantial part of economic activity with finance and infrastructure to facilitate the same. Let's move toward how trade has evolved in the last few decades.

The Current Situation

The Indian economy has been rapidly growing since its liberalisation (in simpler terms, the opening up of the economy for private companies to do business in India with very little government control) in 1990–1991. A slew of reforms was implemented to open the economy, leading to comprehensive growth with a compound annual growth rate (CAGR) of approximately 7 percent[1] in the last 20 years. Besides China, India was by far the fastest growing economy in this period. The rapid growth surge in the last two decades meant that there were rapid changes in the sociocultural milieu. It also meant a fundamental shift in the way Indians were consuming things. For example, Indians started consuming soft drinks such as Coca-Cola and started shopping in big malls much more compared to the pre-1990 era. The trigger for all of this was the economic reforms in 1990, driven largely by increasing trade between India and the rest of the world. An important illustration of this impact is the graph as depicted in Figure 4.1.

FIGURE 4.1: *Trade as a Percentage of GDP Versus Year, 1990–2019*

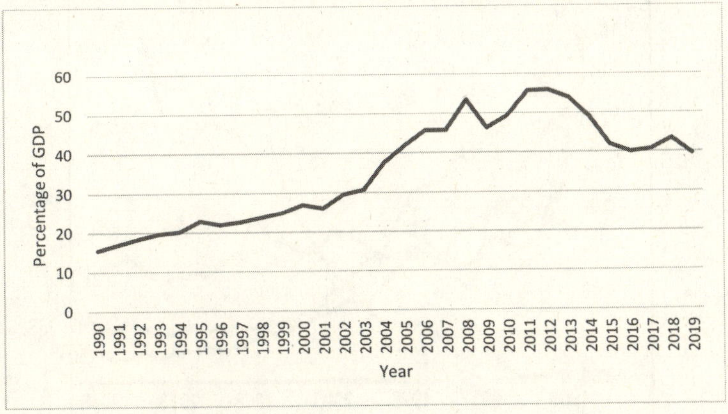

Source: Based on author's analysis of trade data from World Bank Group

[1] IMF Data Analysis.

Trade as a percentage of GDP is a metric that is often measured as an indicator of trade openness in the economy. The trade to GDP percentage has been steadily increasing from 15.67 per cent in 1990, peaking at 55.62 per cent in 2012. Incidentally, it has been declining since 2012 to 39.5 per cent in 2019 according to official records. It's important to note that this threefold increase from 1990 was an important catalyst in the broader Indian growth story as detailed earlier.

Composition of Trade

The composition of trade in terms of exports and imports has been shown in Figure 4.2.

FIGURE 4.2A: *Countrywise Import Partner Share, 1988–2018*

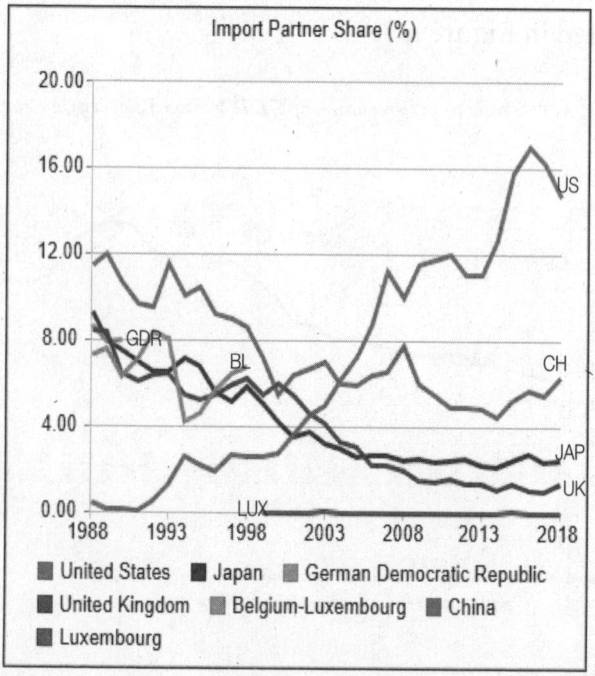

Source: Based on author's analysis of trade data from World Bank Group

FIGURE 4.2B: *Countrywise Export Partner Share, 1988–2018*

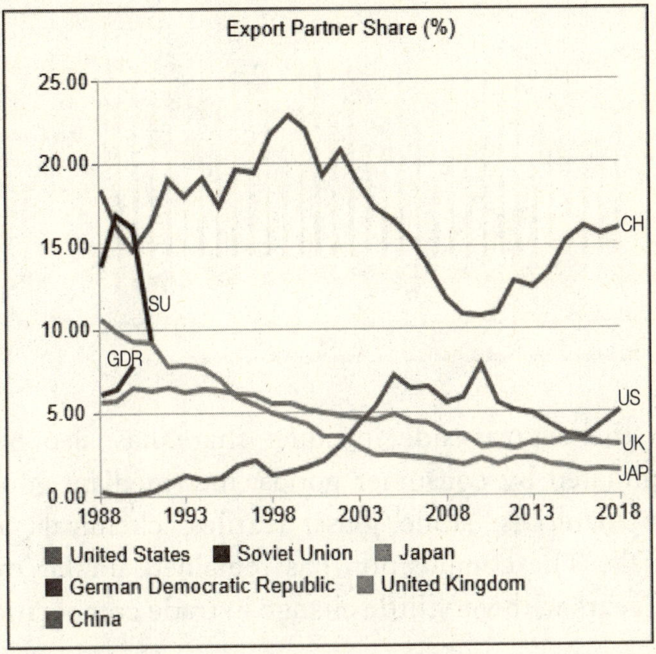

Source: Based on author's analysis of trade data from World Bank Group

As seen in Figures 4.2a and 4.2b, China has leapfrogged as the biggest importer of goods since the early 2000s. It peaked above 16 per cent in 2014 but has been reducing in recent years. Yet it remains by far the single biggest importer of goods and services into India. On the export side, the United States remains the largest export destination for Indian goods and services with a peak of approximately 23 per cent in 1999 and currently at about 15.1 per cent of the overall export share. Interestingly, the exports to China are far lesser than the imports from the country as the data suggests.

The top imports in terms of product share have been raw materials, intermediate goods, consumer and capital goods with little change over the years.

FIGURE 4.3: *India's Top Import Product Share, 1988–2018*

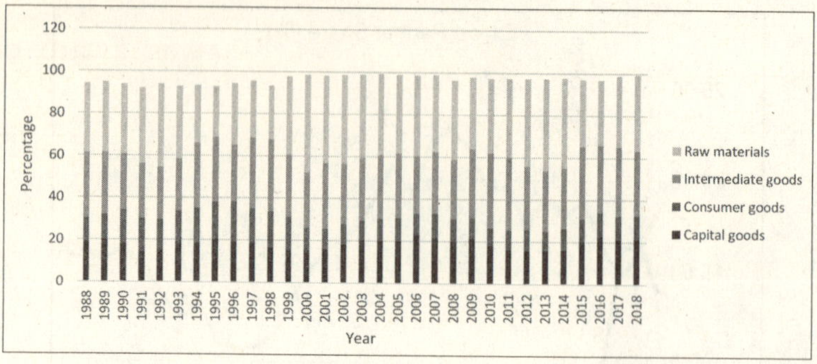

Source: Based on author's analysis of trade data from World Bank Group

On the exports side, product share has also been dominated by consumer goods, intermediate goods, raw materials, stone/glass, textiles, chemicals and metals. The composition has remained similar over the years with very little change in trade composition.

FIGURE 4.4: *India's Top Export Product Share, 1988–2018*

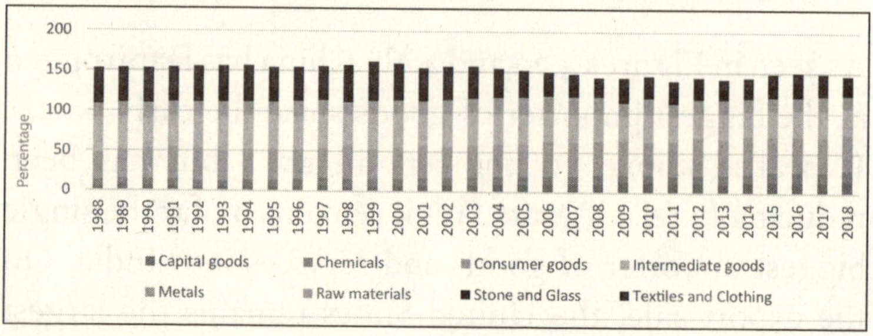

Source: Based on author's analysis of trade data from World Bank Group

What does this mean? We tend to export more consumer goods (examples include items such as milk, furniture and television) and intermediate goods to the rest of the world whereas most of our imports are either raw materials or intermediate goods from other countries.

The composition of capital goods (example of machinery on a factory floor) and consumer goods in the overall import basket is much lower than the raw materials and intermediate goods.

Is free trade always a good thing? This is an important question: Is it always good that we get an iPhone made in Cupertino when it is launched? Is it always good that we get Fiji apples in our supermarkets and cocoa chocolates from Africa? The answer, like in most things in economics, is that it depends. The literature on this subject is complex and it could be a book in itself. Unfettered free trade, where any international player can sell in our domestic markets without any regulations, has its shortcomings. There are possibilities for big players (such as Coca-Cola or Walmart) to come into India and become monopolies due to their large size and monetary strength. This could further alienate small and medium enterprises (SMEs) in the country that predominantly constitutes an informal economy that accounts for more than 85 per cent of employment[2] in the non-agriculture economy of the country.

On the other hand, you need free trade to expand the 'pie' (greater variety of products such as phones, merchandise, clothing, etc.) to increase the standards of living in the country. In a rapidly growing country such as India, which tends to adopt export-driven models, free trade is needed to boost exports which, in turn, improves domestic competitiveness (the ability

[2] https://www.ilo.org/wcmsp5/groups/public/---ed_emp/---ifp_skills/documents/publication/wcms_734503.pdf

of domestic firms to produce more goods in line with international standards). Experts have vacillated between the two ends of the trade divide but the truth is perhaps somewhere in the middle. In simpler terms, there needs to be a fine balance between opening up too much and too little for a country like India.

In this context, assuming that it could be sensible for India to accelerate its trade avenues through greater exports and a more competitive domestic market, how can that be done within the constraints of India's complex economy? Here are some possibilities through the Kautilyan lens.

Kautilyan Tantra on Trade

Enhancing the Ease of Trading Goods

The idea of enhancing the ease of trading goods and reducing barriers for free and fair trade was conceptualised by Kautilya. The panyadaksha (trade commissioner) played an important role in providing regulatory oversight and intervened when required—sort of a Keynesian intervention when needed.

Kautilya's focus was to ensure that the customers' priorities were at the forefront in the implementation of policy. These include price stability, ease of trading between partners and the state playing an intermediary oversight role. In other words, 'there was a definite attempt to strike a reasonable balance between the interests of the state, the traders and the customers', as Kangle mentions (1965, 176).

Kautilyan Tantra

Kautilya advocated for free and fair trade of all goods and services across the value spectrum and production quantities.

He seemed to be clear on the notion of free and fair trade for all goods and services across the value spectrum and production quantities. He had a sense of understanding that trade was always a good thing within and outside the country. For example, he mentions that 'pearls could be imported from Ceylon (Sri Lanka), aloe from Burma, woolen clothes from Nepal, furs and horses from Gandahara (Afghanistan) and Vanayu from Persia' (Sihag 2014).

Furthermore, incentives were provided—especially for imports—to improve the ease of 'access to trading'. For example, duties were completely exempted for shippers and caravans who came into the country so that they could maximise profit. Moreover, they were also provided immunity from legal issues—except for their partners and associates—related to financial matters. Even tariffs, where applicable, were broadly streamlined across all products.

So how does this apply to our current scenario? Much of the dialogue in recent times has been around enhancing 'ease of doing business'.

One of the things that countries do is to reduce the number of trade barriers and enhance the ease of trading goods. For example, countries look at improving 'ease of doing business' to make it more attractive for other countries to trade with them. India's recent improvement in the World Bank Group's 'Doing Business Rankings' from the 100th position in 2017 to 63rd in 2020 is welcome.[3]

An important area which can be improved upon is 'trading across borders', where India remains at 68th position. The costs and the time delays in overcoming regulatory barriers (restrictions on free movements of goods and services) are among the most important things to address if India has to further improve. As Kautilya suggests, if the focus was primarily on the customer and incentives are provided to trading partners (import and export preferences), then trading across borders can be enhanced. Moreover, the streamlining of tariffs/duties to a fixed amount across product portfolios also helps to boost the ease of business among trading partners. The emphasis on simplifying the trading structure with the state playing the role of enabling commerce, which is the Kautilyan way, would help in making trade policy more effective.

Internal Trade between States

Kautilya promoted the internal movement of goods and services. He believed that the movement of goods from

[3] https//www.doingbusiness.org/en/data/exploreeconomies/india. Even though the prospective rankings have been discontinued recently due to data discrepancies for some countries besides India, India's ranking and data analysis remain valid for retrospective analysis.

Kashmir to Kanyakumari could be a huge economic catalyst for the kingdom. The Kautilyan state took various steps to promote this, as highlighted in the Kautilyan Tantra:

Kautilyan Tantra

Promotion of internal trade within the Mauryan Empire was highlighted through the following examples:

1. Traders moved in caravans (sartha सार्थ) in groups due to safety concerns. The state took extra steps to provide insurance cover for goods to move from point A to point B within the empire through a marginal cess called vartani (वर्तनि).
2. Standardisation of weights and measurements was done across the empire by the pautavadhyaksa (पौतवाध्यक्ष) to ensure that time and costs were saved by traders carrying out their activities. It was aimed at promoting 'ease of trade' within the empire.
3. Large sections of the bureaucracy were focused on ensuring these actions are followed up. These include bringing together panyadhyaksa (पण्याध्यक्ष), samsthadhyaksa (संस्थध्यक्ष), vaidharna (वैधरण), rajapanya (राजपण्य) and parabhumija (परभूमिष्ठ) to work on promoting trade within the empire.

Boosting internal trade between states has been one of the least prioritised areas to drive growth in India. Even though the goods and services tax (GST) has been implemented, there needs to be a much more streamlined mechanism to ease trade within the country's borders and between states, as research on internal migration in India reinforces (Kone, Liu, Mattoo, Özdena, et al 2017). The research mentions that the 'migration between neighbouring districts in the same state is at least 50 per cent more than migration between districts which are on different sides of a state border'. The innumerable regulatory blocks within states and the permits required for doing trade also need to be eliminated for trade to proceed forward.

Furthermore, sectoral regulatory constraints need to be eased as well. The government's recent efforts to scrap the APMCE Act and the three legislations (Chikarmane 2020) to open the agricultural sector are steps aligned with the Kautilyan worldview. The ability for farmers to freely sell their produce across states and sectors with the central government providing an oversight role—similar to enforcing matsya nyaya to ensure big players don't dominate over the small farmers—is perhaps the appropriate way forward for expanding the large domestic market for trade in India.

As Kautilya cleverly articulated in his time, internal open trade provides a huge domestic market for trading participants. As he articulated earlier, the expansion of a large domestic market will have a ripple effect on enhanced exports and greater external trade with the rest of the world. Not only will this boost the trade-to-GDP ratios in the longer run, but it will also ensure that the domestic players are not left out of the broader trade trajectory. It would help to address some of the challenges mentioned in the earlier section on free trade in this chapter.

Export Diversification and Tariff Management

One of the important recent trends in trade in India has been the similar portfolio of imports and exports over the last thirty years. Despite many economic reforms, while the quantity of trade increased (how many goods we trade), the composition remains the same as highlighted in the preceding sections of this chapter. This is particularly the case in the export sector since export diversification is one of the key strategies that many low-income countries have used to boost growth. It would help for us to look at Kautilya's thinking on this. He suggested the need to have a very diversified export portfolio both from a product and value standpoint. He wanted to have 'a combination of high and low-value goods' which are diverse so that one doesn't rely too much on a particular product. This is very relevant especially in this post-pandemic economy that we are dealing with where 'atmanirbartha' (self-resilience) plays an important role.

In a world increasingly being dominated by trade wars[4] and the competition between countries to manage their local tariffs for products, tariff management becomes an important subject. According to Kautilya, rigid tariffs aren't the best way forward and there needs to be a certain level of flexibility in their implementation.

[4] A trade war is what happens when one country retaliates against another by raising import or export tariffs or placing other restrictions on the opposing country's import or export tariffs.

The sense that one gets is that he doesn't see this as an economic tool but rather a supplementary revenue generator. Interestingly, he prefers 'ease of trading' to be more important than the tariffs being a geopolitical tool or a revenue-generating monolith.

> **Kautilyan Tantra**
>
> Risk management through product diversification: Despite his support for trade, he had a pragmatic approach. He emphasised having a 'combination of high value and low-value goods'. An optimal mix of goods and services was intended so that the risk taken for high-value goods was sufficient yet not excessive. On the other hand, he also recognised the need for high-value goods to boost revenue at a much faster rate than low-value goods. The mix of these goods led him to also advocate for product diversification—urging his citizens to produce a wide variety of products so that there is no over-reliance on one of them.

GOLD MONETISATION—IDEAS AND SOLUTIONS

Can you name an asset that is purchased by almost all Indian households? Irrespective of region, class, caste or religion, the demand for gold is consistent among Indian consumers. No matter what the economic environment is, the neighbourhood jewellers are always glittering—whether it is Kalyan, GRT Jewellers or Tanishq, the demand for gold is continuous. This is despite the fact that economists (myself included) tend to form the view that gold is not a productive asset and there are other forms of investment that are more productive.

This craze for gold can be easily explained if you pay attention to your grandmother's perspective. My late grandmother's consumer choices are a classic example. When I was born, she bought a gold bracelet as an investment and deposited it in a bank locker. This compounded in value over subsequent years and reaped good dividends in the long term. Not only did she use it for my marriage, but she also made sure every other sibling was accorded the same privilege.

When I probed her further on her investment choices as a housewife, her answers were pragmatic (like all householders are). Given her limited resources, she felt that the best investment was in gold since there was not only an assurance that gold provided in terms of monetary returns, but it also provided sentimental value which was far more than the monetary value. The sentimental value of the ornament, when used many years later, reflected how much she had saved and how much the family progressed economically over the years. It was a symbol of progress through thrift and hard work, in her view. This represents the Indian householder's worldview, which, in my opinion, runs the 'feminine' Indian economy. It also serves as a form of social mobility for individuals like my grandmother who were in the lower-income spectrum.

Many individuals below the middle-income threshold and even those below the poverty line (BPL) do not have access to formal credit channels for personal and professional investments. In that context, many of them depend on reliable assets like gold as a form of assurance and a catalyst for social mobility—the movement from low- to middle- or high-income families in the social structure (Churiwel and Shreni 2012). Moreover, this also serves as an important barter for millions of migrants who move from state to state within the country (Kundu 2019).

Hence, unlike in other countries, the appetite for gold in India is a unique combination of expected material returns for the metal, the sentimental value of the actual ornament, and the utility value that it serves in Indian customs and rituals such as marriages, religious functions and other social gatherings. Among people, it has held a consistently increasing space in their asset portfolios and life choices over the years. On the other hand, the role of gold hasn't garnered enough attention in policy circles. This is perhaps the most startling example of a 'policy disconnect' between policymakers and the realities/trends on the ground. While the world moved away from the gold standard in the 1970s, the economic dynamic around the accumulation of gold is still very relevant in Indian households. However, not much has been done to analyse and provide solutions, except for a few recent initiatives, which we will discuss later in the chapter.

It's important to note that we are referring to the household consumption/savings of gold and not that in temples or other public institutions. With this caveat, in this section, I hope to explore the background data on gold accumulation, its impact on the real economy, some of the efforts taken by governments to address this and possible solutions to utilise it to boost the Indian economy. We also try to decipher Kautilya's views on such public assets and their role in ensuring economic prosperity for society.

Historical Context

Gold has always been a barometer of wealth in Indian society. Well before even the *Arthashastra*, various Puranas mention gold as a benchmark for economic success and prosperity. While its value might have reduced after the invention of paper currency and financial markets in recent years, its perception in people's minds as a safe asset is significant. To understand the Indian story, we need to understand how gold demand functions in the global context. So, what are the components of gold demand in the world?

FIGURE 4.5: *Types of Gold Demand, 2010–2020*

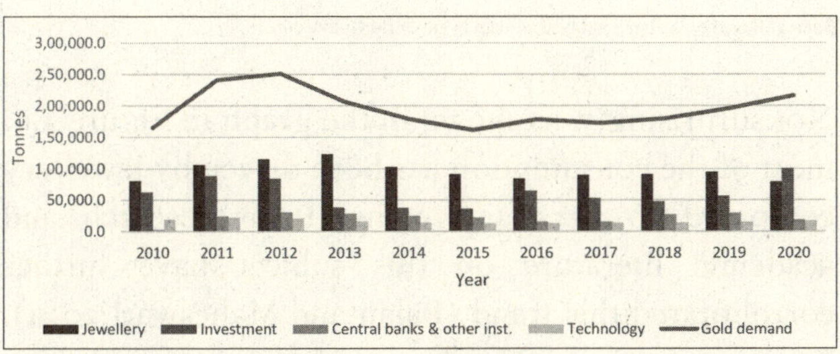

Source: Based on author's analysis of data from World Gold Council

As seen in Figure 4.5, demand for gold is largely divided into the sub-categories shown in the graph. Jewellery and investment (majorly bar and coin purchases) are the two biggest drivers of growth in the international market followed by technology and central bank purchases. While the consumption of jewellery, between 2,000 and 2,750 tonnes, has been robust, the demand for investment has been declining since its peak in 2012. This translates into people buying more personalised jewellery that is worn in our weddings and religious functions and casually as well when compared to individuals who buy gold bars purely for the sake of investment. In this context, how does Indian demand fair?

FIGURE 4.6: *Composition of Gold Consumption in India, 2010–2020*

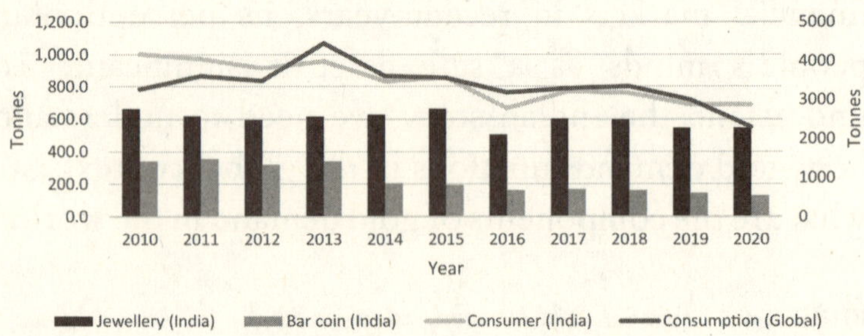

Source: Based on author's analysis of data from World Gold Council

Not surprisingly, as shown in the graph in Figure 4.6, most of the consumption has been driven by jewellery compared to bars and coins. Prior research and academic literature on this subject have further corroborated this trend (Balaji and Maheswari 2014). This gap between jewellery and bars and coins has been increasing since 2010, though the quantum of total consumption has been declining since then. Given Indian households and women's preference to use jewellery as an asset as well as a luxury item, it isn't surprising that it is the highest component of Indian gold consumption.

As per Figure 4.7, India and China have been two of the world's highest consumers of gold. While India was consuming more in the earlier part of the decade, since 2012, the Chinese have been increasing their consumption and hold a steady lead over India.

FIGURE 4.7: *Gold Consumption Data, 2010–2020*

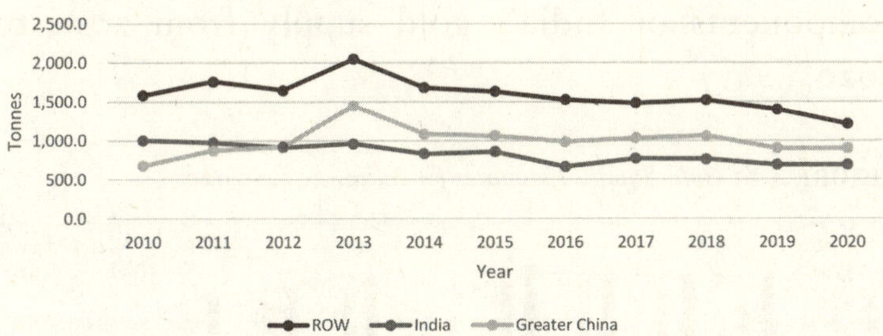

Source: Based on author's analysis of data from World Gold Council

The reduction in the growth of gold consumption could be due to the decreasing growth rates in recent years. The year 2012 seems to have been an inflexion point for gold consumption with respect to India and China. Since 2012, China's consumption of gold has been higher than India's. While there are many reasons for this, we focus on the Indian story in this section within the broader global context.

The consumption of gold in India reached a peak of $49.2 billion in 2011 and has declined since to stabilise at around $30.9 billion in 2019. In simpler terms, in

2019, the market for gold in India was about $30.9 billion, which is approximately 18 per cent of the global market in 2019 (a slightly lesser percentage in 2020). Logically speaking, this huge market should be a boon for gold manufacturers in India since there is a robust market for gold consistently over the years.

However, that's assuming that we have the capacity to produce all the gold that is needed for consumption in the country. Given that gold constitutes more than ⅓rd of India's imports every year, prima facie there is surely a gap in domestic gold production. This is illustrated further in Figure 4.8, which highlights the components of India's gold supply from 2012 to 2020.

FIGURE 4.8: *Gold Supply Estimates for India, 2012–2020*

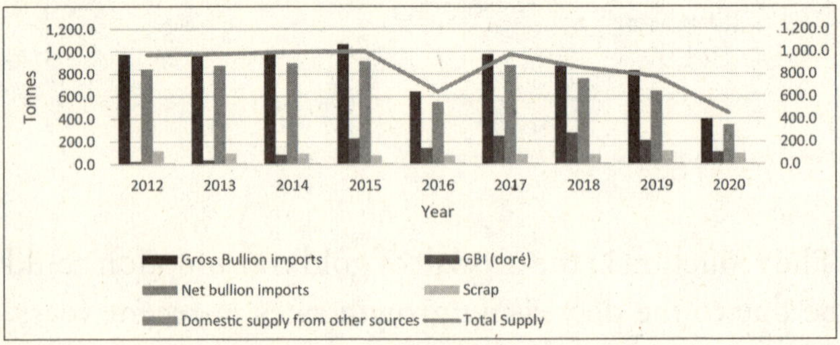

Source: Based on author's analysis of data from World Gold Council

As seen in Figure 4.8, more than 80–90 per cent of gold consumed in India is imported. The amount of domestic gold production is negligible compared to the amount imported into the country. When compared to other countries, the import dependency is far higher. The demand-supply ratios from domestic production are shown in Figure 4.9.

FIGURE 4.9: *Domestic Production/Consumer Demand Ratio, 2010–2019*

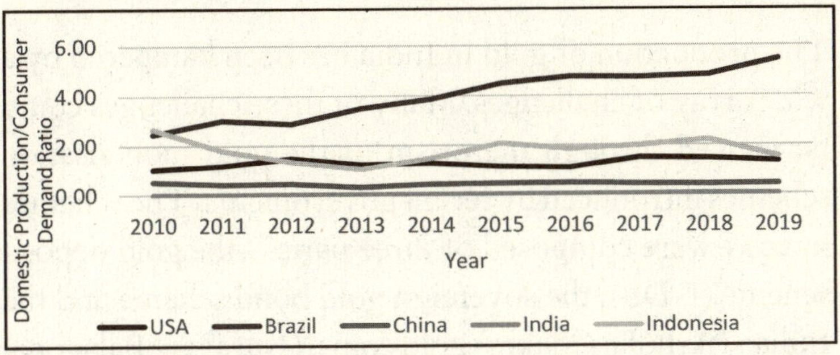

[5]

Source: Based on author's analysis of data from World Gold Council

Figure 4.9 illustrates the huge differences between domestic gold production and consumption. All the comparative countries have higher ratios than India. While Brazil has the highest ratio, countries like the USA, China and Indonesia fall in the 0.4–2.21 range. It is reasonable to see high import dependency on some products but in this case, we are completely dependent on imports for our gold demand. Given that we are one of the biggest consumers of gold, this negligible domestic production could create huge import

[5] Volume of fine gold material contained in the doré. Domestic supply from local mine production, recovery from imported copper concentrates and disinvestment. Total supply can be consumed across three sectors—jewellery, investment and technology. Consequently, the total supply value in Figure 4.10 will not add to jewellery plus investment demand for India.

dependencies along with reduced influence in the global gold market.

Challenges Involved in Domestic Gold Production

The production of gold in India has been hampered by a wide array of challenges. Many of these challenges could be viewed through the prism of the gold monetisation schemes introduced by recent governments. The schemes in 2015 were composed of three parts—the gold deposit scheme (GDS), the sovereign gold bond scheme and the Indian (Ashoka Chakra) gold coins. (Narayan, Balagopal and Sahay 2015) For the sake of brevity and focus, we zoom in on the largest and most significant part of the monetisation exercise by looking at the GDS scheme.

Gold Deposit Scheme (GDS)

The GDS scheme is the only scheme that allows the physical collection of gold from individuals. Customers can deposit gold through three main maturities—short (1–3 years), medium (5–7 years) and long (12–15 years) term. Customers are required to verify the authenticity of the gold at the collection and purity testing centre (CPTC); the bank subsequently does the same with its own refiner once the gold is deposited and then issues a certificate to the customers. After the maturity period is over, customers can redeem their certificate for gold bars or the monetary equivalent at market prices. It is important to note here that customers don't receive the exact gold that had been deposited. This scheme was further modified by the RBI in 2019 and renamed the Revamped Gold Deposit Scheme (R-GDS) with some changes to the original scheme. This was further modified in 2021 with some minimal changes to the original scheme.[6]

Despite the possible attractive benefits of the scheme, both for the customer and the bank (and, as an extension, the state, in the case of state-owned banks), the scheme failed badly after it was introduced in 2015. As of 2018, only about 0.0024 per cent of the overall household and temple gold was collected (Singh and Sasi, 2018). This was primarily caused by the following challenges which also plague the gold industry on a macro level. These are segregated into the various stakeholders in the ecosystem for the sake of convenience and analysis.

1. Refiners and collection and purity testing centres (CPTCs)

   According to a 2019 study, there were about 15 refiners and over 300 CPTCs that had been used for the scheme. One of the major challenges has been scale and the development of necessary infrastructure to accelerate the refining and testing of gold. Due to the small number of customers, the scalability is very low for investment in these schemes. On the other hand, while the CPTCs are greater in number than refiners, they are smaller in scale and additional investment in infrastructure is likely to be expensive for them.

[6] https://sbi.co.in/web/personal-banking/investments-deposits/govt-schemes/gold-banking/revamped-gold-deposit-scheme-r-gds

Moreover, for the customers who are used to going to jewellery shops to get an estimate of the value of gold, it requires a structural change to go to the CPTCs instead. It also makes CPTCs less attractive compared to jewellery shops where the direct sale of jewellery also takes place.

2. Financial institutions

The banks are also affected by the scale factor mentioned in the preceding point. Most bankers do not pay attention to expanding this scheme since the number of deposits is very low. This indicates that bankers do not attach high priority to this for their business and most staff aren't well versed with the scheme due to its perceived lack of importance. Furthermore, in some sections of the banks, there seems to be a mismatch between the maturity of the gold metal loans (six months) and gold deposit loans (three years), further disincentivising the GDS scheme among bankers. The average wait time for the customer is at best seven days given the best CPTC facilities whereas the same can be done in a jewellery shop in a few minutes. In addition, banks can't facilitate in-house CPTCs (as proposed by the refiners) to fast-track the process due to their lack of expertise. These factors allude to the fact that bankers are not only disincentivised, but they also seem to be not in control of the end-end process of the scheme.

3. Consumers

From the consumer point of view, the availability of gold loans, their much shorter approval process and ease of transaction make them more attractive. The process of going to a CPTC and the subsequent verification process makes the entire investment laborious. Most importantly, due to the sentimental value attached to gold in India, the fact that after the maturity period ends, consumers aren't getting back the same gold that they had invested makes it less attractive to them as an investment proposition.

Given the contours of the demand-supply dynamics of India and the structural challenges, as observed in the GDS scheme, it will be wise to look at how Kautilya's thinking might provide solutions to turn gold into a viable investment that can assuage all the stakeholders in the gold ecosystem.

Kautilyan Tantra on Gold Monetisation

Consumer Is King

Kautilya eloquently ideated in numerous instances that the 'consumer is king', and he would, in all likelihood, use that as a reference point for his solution to gold monetisation. This approach would fundamentally change the orientation of gold development in favour of the consumer. For instance, one of the main drawbacks of the GDS has been that the Indian consumer wanted the same gold that he/she had surrendered to be given back to them at the end of the maturity period. Due to the sentimental value attached to the ornament, consumers are keen to invest in bonds only if they can have the option of getting the same ornament back. In this regard, Kautilya's view of 'consumer being king' serves very well.

In this case, the customised gold being exchanged by consumers, through the GDS scheme, could be more successful if the exact or similar gold ornament was returned, to retain the authenticity and sentimental value of the purchases. As Kautilya mentions, not only will this protect consumer interests, it will also expand the scope of the scheme to benefit the country.

Kautilyan Tantra

Kautilya's view on consumer preferences to be supreme in economic policymaking discussions is illustrated in the quote:

'The smiths shall return to the customer the same quantity of precious metal, of identical quality, as was entrusted to him, even if the customer claims it after a lapse of time' (2.14.5, 6).

02.14.05 यथावर्णप्रमाणं निक्षेपं गृह्णीयुः तथाविधं एवार्पयेयुः
02.14.06 कालान्तराद् अपि च तथाविधं एव प्रतिगृह्णीयुः, अन्यत्र क्षीणपरिशीर्णाभ्याम्

Kautilya always viewed the transactional nature of banking operations as focused on the consumer. There is an inherent belief in protecting the consumer's interests, especially when ornaments and commodities were exchanged or bartered, as in the case of gold here. His primary motivation seemed to be that consumer choices determined the success of any commercial transaction.

Coordinated Supply Chain

Kautilya would have advocated the need for coordination at the supply end of things to boost economic activity. This is even more pertinent in the context of the gold supply in India. One of the critiques of the GDS and broader gold supply in India is that there is very little coordination between stakeholders in the supply ecosystem. In simpler terms, it is the lack of coordination between refiners, CPTCs and financial institutions, which we had discussed in the preceding section.

Kautilya could advocate a similar approach to the issue of lack of supply coordination in gold production. For example, there a centralised organisation can be created that helps to bring together the refiners, CPTCs and financial institutions to ensure greater coordination. This could be a national entity that tries to promote the interests of the stakeholders in the gold production system. This entity could ensure there is seamless coordination for more efficient outcomes.

Kautilyan Tantra

Kautilya's view on 'supply schedule', which refers to a coordinated supply chain, can be interpreted in a few ways. Though there hasn't been an explicit mention of this in the terms that we understand today, there has been an emphasis on the thinking in the text, as evidenced in the quote:

'An agent selling goods on behalf of someone else, at the right time and place (i.e. realizing the best price), shall hand over to the owner of the merchandise the price as received (the cost price + profit made) (less their commission) … If the price falls (between the time of entrusting goods and the time of sale), only the lower prize realized shall be payable' (Sihag 2014, 63).

03.12.03 उपनिधिभोक्ता देशकालानुरूपं भोगवेतनं दद्यात्, द्वादशपणं च दण्डम्

03.12.04 उपभोगनिमित्तं नष्टं विनष्टं वाऽभ्यावहेत्, चतुर्विंशतिपणश्च दण्डः, अन्यथा वा निष्पतने

Leveraging Market Power

Market power is another important metric that Kautilya wanted to leverage to his empire's advantage. In the global gold markets, India is one of the leading consumers of gold yet is nowhere near in terms of production unlike countries such as China. To expand its presence and utilise its consumer potential, Kautilya, to tackle the current scenario, might suggest that it will be prudent for India to capitalise on this market power to boost its presence in the global markets and increase its domestic production capacity.

Kautilyan Tantra

Kautilya's view on market power is relevant to the suggestion mentioned. The importance of strength and power—mostly in a geopolitical context but it can be applied to market power as well—is highlighted at various stages of the text, as seen in one of his key quotes:

'A mighty king can get the help of another energetic one or he can hire or buy more fighters' (Shamasastry 1915, 337).

09.1.07 प्रभाववान् उत्साहवन्तं राजानं प्रभावेनातिसन्धत्ते तद्विशिष्टं अन्यं राजानं आवाह्य भृत्वा क्रीत्वा प्रवीरपुरुषान्

Being one of the biggest consumers of gold, India has a considerable advantage of consumer power in the global markets. This is a position of market strength which India could leverage significantly to ensure that much of the global market movements are in India's favour. This could be used to enhance its domestic production capacity to gain a greater share in the producers' markets as well.

SAVINGS, INVESTMENT AND GROWTH

One of the most important economic concepts is the dynamic between savings and investment and the role played by savings to boost investment in the economy. Along with other similar Asian economies, India's savings rate has been relatively high in recent years. This has been attributed to a variety of socio-economic factors along with rising income levels, especially in the last two decades post liberalisation. In this section, we hope to explore the Kautilyan approach to savings—along with the general characteristics of the Indian savings dynamic—and how this approach can boost the growth story in the future.

Literature on the Linkages between Savings, Investment and Growth

The literature on the role of savings in driving growth has been evolving. In the 1950s, Solow's approach (1956) focused on the rate of technical change (technology), the savings ratio and the rate of population growth as determinants of the rate of the steady growth of the economy. These are further bolstered by the assumption that all savings are automatically invested and translated into output growth under wage-price flexibility and full employment. In addition, recent endogenous growth models have linked modes of investment to affect long-run growth by making the rate of technical change and productivity growth linked either to the accumulation of physical capital or human capital in the long run (Romer 1986; Lucas 1988).

Additional research has shown that accumulating physical capital is the major driver of long-term economic growth (Barro 1990). Some research work has also indicated that there is a tendency to increase the savings rate within low-income countries as they grow, yet it starts reducing as the country becomes a higher-income country with better per capita income levels (Ogaki, Ostry and Reinhart 1996). In the case of India, some recent literature that looks at the specific relationship between savings and investment in recent years showcases a long-run equilibrium relationship between savings and investment in the country (Mishra, Das and Mishra 2010). Moreover, additional literature suggests that savings drive investment in India and that investment isn't necessarily the engine of growth (Verma 2007).

Mythical Growth Theories

India's very moderate growth in the early 1960s and 1970s was labelled the 'Hindu rate of growth' by some academics. This trend was started by economist Raj Krishna in the early 1970s, inspired by historians such as Max Weber. This hypothesis argued that India's growth was averaging around 3 per cent mainly because the Hindus, who are almost 80 per cent of the Indian population, were believers in rebirth and due to this, they were restrained in spending and were more inclined to save. Hence, their religious beliefs were contrarian to the Protestant ethic that Max Weber prophesied as the central catalyst of the Industrial Revolution.

This was further picked up by academics who used this profusely without much evidence for such theories. As illustrated earlier (in the Introduction), this was despite the fact that even Vedic sages had mentioned that artha (wealth creation) was one of the components of purusharthas, which were integral for any human being's progress. Moreover, this seems to be more virtue signalling that doesn't stand when tested against evidence and facts.

FIGURE 4.10: *World GDP from 0 CE to 1700 CE, by Angus Maddison*

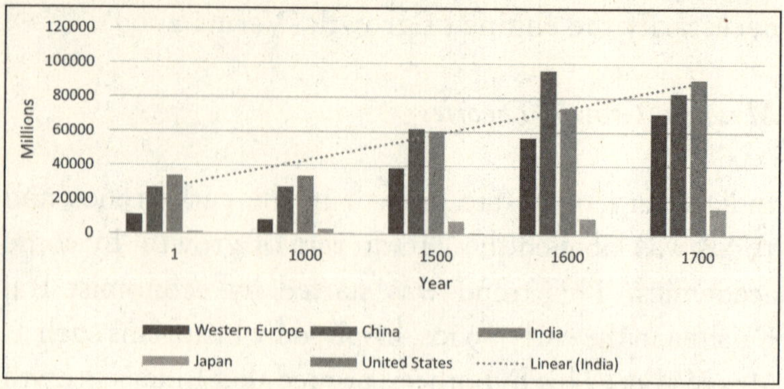

Source: Based on author's analysis of data from *The World Economy: Historical Statistics* by Angus Maddison[7]

Figure 4.10 shows the GDP[8] growth over the last 1,700 years. It's interesting to note that till 1600, India and China have been exchanging their positions at the top of the GDP charts on average every 500 years. Furthermore, till 1700, the Western countries played a marginal role in global economic activity. During the time of India's dominance before the British rule, the Hindu population of the country was the same, if not higher. Some critics might argue that this position as a global economic leader was mainly due to the role of large populations since production capacity was nascent in those years.

Yet from 1990 onwards, India grew at an average of 5.5 per cent during the first decade, 7.6 per cent in the second decade and 6.7 per cent during the last decade. In the last 30 years, India has become one of the

7 http//www.ggdc.net/maddison/oriindex.htm

8 According to the IMF, the GDP measures the monetary value of final goods and services—that is, those that are bought by the final user—produced in a country in a given period (say a quarter or a year).

largest-growing emerging markets. Was India less Hindu during this period in comparison to the time when Raj Krishna commented on this? Of course not. This had nothing to do with the characteristics of the majority community but rather with a socialistic economic system that was inefficient and regressive. The reforms in the 1990s served to springboard the growth story that we see today. It is important to highlight this point and show the evidence of such growth theories for the readers to make their conclusions.

Kautilyan Perspective on Investment and Savings

Kautilyan Factometer

Kautilya's views on savings and investment are clear. He views the need to boost private investment as one of the key drivers of growth, along with the accumulation of capital. While the role of the markets wasn't structurally present then, much of this accumulation points to the aggregation of external and internal wealth in the country. The external wealth is mainly driven by state revenue whereas the internal wealth is primarily driven by household savings. Moreover, the Kautilyan worldview also extended to the utility value/conversion of wealth accumulation to wealth creation. He believed that the 'root of wealth is economic activity ... and a king achieving those objectives by creating productive economic activity' (Rangarajan 1992). This essentially translates to the modern-day view of the transmission between savings to investment from both the public and private sectors. The Kautilyan perspective of keeping the focus on economic activity through the pillars of productivity, conversion of savings into investment and robust governance mechanisms is something that even modern policymakers would agree with.

Composition of Indian Savings—Trends and Segmentation

Composition of Overall Indian Savings

The context of Indian savings in recent years is shown in Figure 4.11 (NAS 2021).

FIGURE 4.11: *Gross Savings by Institutional Sectors, 2011–2021*

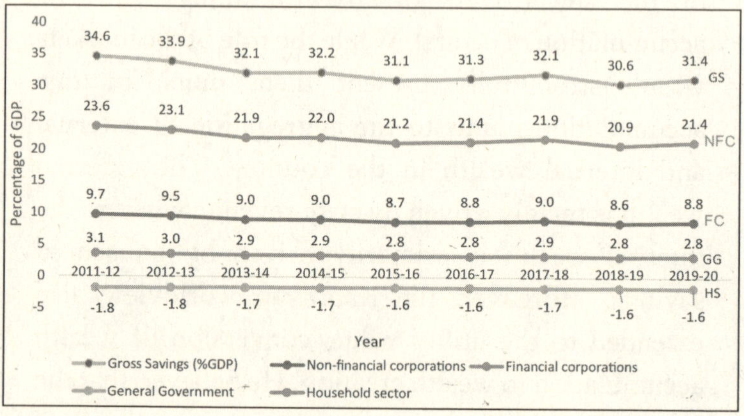

Source: Based on author's analysis of data from *National Accounts Statistics* 2021

As seen in Figure 4.11, the overall Indian savings rate has been ranging from a high of 34.6 per cent of GDP in 2011–2012 to 31.4 per cent in 2019–2020 with a moderate decline through these years. It is important to note that the role of domestic households is substantial within this; it contributed to almost 23.6 per cent of GDP in 2011–2012 with a gradual decline to 21.4 per cent in 2019–2020. This is followed by the non-financial corporations, which had a decrease in contribution towards domestic savings from 9.7 per cent in 2011–2012 to about 8.8 per cent in 2019–2020, followed by financial corporations, which reduced from 3.1 per cent in 2011–2012 to approximately 2.8 per cent in 2019–2020. Unlike the popular narrative, the contribution of household savings is very integral to the broader savings story with very little contribution from the financial corporations.

A cross-sectional comparison with other countries on gross national savings as a percentage of GDP provides a better perspective on Indian savings in a global context. The overall gross savings is shown in Figure 4.14.

FIGURE 4.12: *Gross Savings as a Percentage of GDP, 1980–2024 (Estimate)*

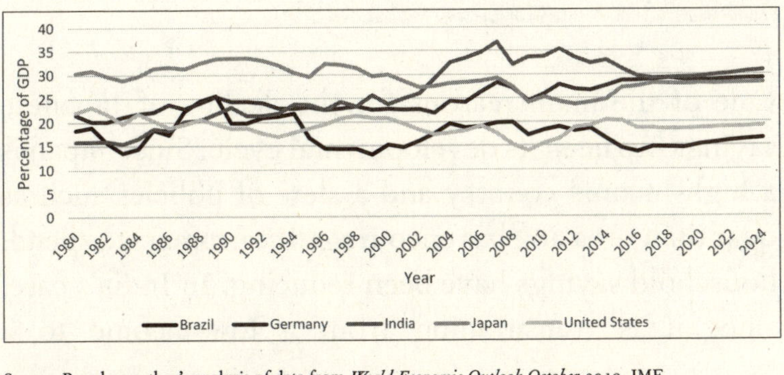

Source: Based on author's analysis of data from *World Economic Outlook October 2019*, IMF

There are two key observations that one can make from these cross-country comparisons. First, India has one of the highest gross savings rates in the world followed by Germany, Japan, the USA and Brazil in recent years. India's gross savings rates started accelerating around 2003 when the boom phase of the Indian economy started picking up. An increase in income has had a corresponding increase in gross savings for the country. Second, the composition of households to the broader savings story is the highest in India. In Japan, there has been a consistent decline in household savings over the years, as shown in Figure 4.13, which are being replaced by corporate savings.

FIGURE 4.13: *Japan's Household Savings Ratio, 1994–2018*

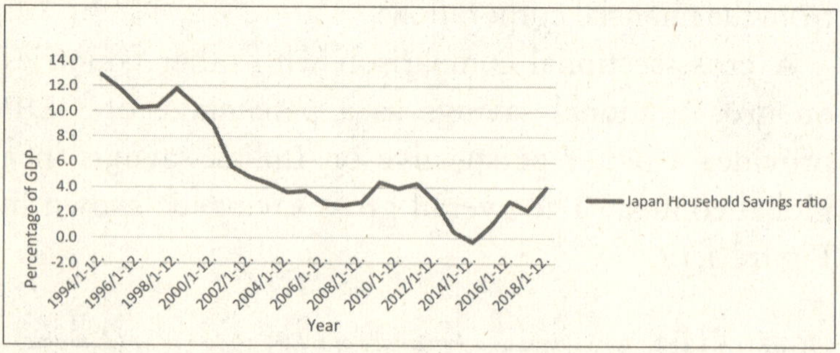

Source: Based on author's analysis of data from *National Accounts of Japan 2020*

One of the main reasons for the decline of Japanese savings has been its developmental cycle. Since Japan is a high-income country and a slew of policies such as quantitative easing has encouraged consumers to spend, household savings have been reducing. In India's case, since it is transitioning from a low-income to a middle-income country, it is bound to have a higher savings rate compared to developed countries.

Composition of Household Savings

The composition of the household savings sector provides a more nuanced understanding of the factors at play. According to the Household Finance Committee Report (Gopalakrishnan, Mathur, Rath, Vats and Ramodorai 2017), the average household has 77 per cent of its total assets in real estate, 7 per cent in other durable goods (such as vehicles, livestock and poultry, agricultural machinery and non-farm business equipment), 11 per cent in gold and the residual 5 per cent in financial assets (such as deposits and savings accounts, publicly traded shares, mutual funds, life insurance and retirement accounts). The data from NAS 2019 provides a more granular analysis of the composition.

FIGURE 4.14: *Household Savings Composition, 2011–2016*

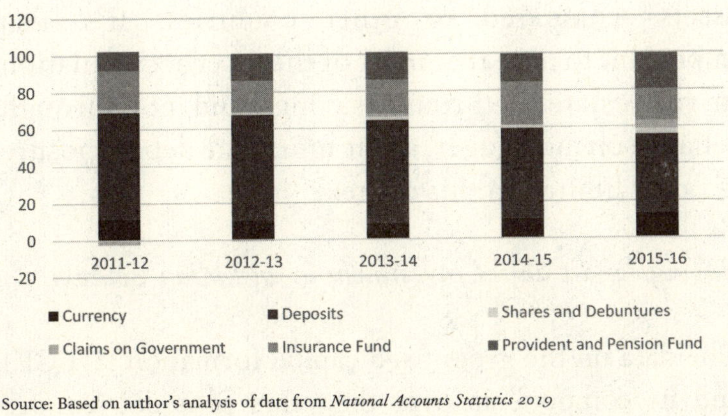

Source: Based on author's analysis of date from *National Accounts Statistics 2019*

The cross-sectional comparison of other similar countries and India provides a much better overview of the dynamics of the household sector (Badarinza, Balasubramanian and Ramadorai 2019). Figure 4.15 illustrates the same.

FIGURE 4.15: *Countrywise Allocation of Household Balance Sheets Based on Goods and Debt*

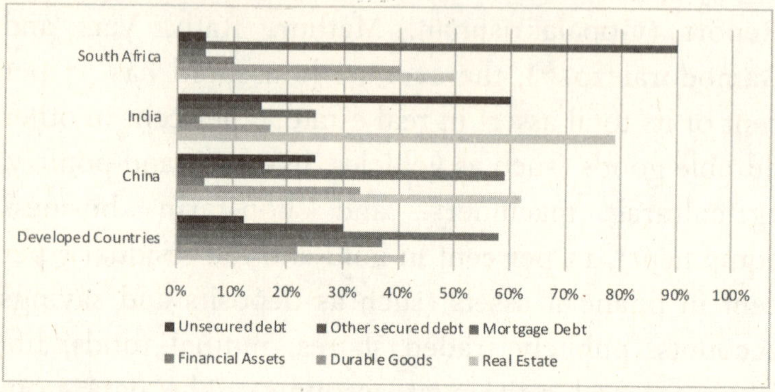

Source: Based on author's analysis of data from Badarinza, Balasubramanian and Ramadorai 2019

In terms of household savings composition, India has the highest asset allocation to real estate—followed by durable goods and financial assets—compared to other countries. It's also important to note that most of the asset accumulation in real estate is through savings and not through reliance on mortgages, as the mortgage debt exposure is fairly limited in this context.

Savings and Capital Investment in an Indian Context

The data on the gross fixed capital formation (GFCF) and its components over the years provides a more definitive perspective on the potential of the household sector to drive the investment agenda in the years to come. Figure 4.16 shows the details.

FIGURE 4.16: *Gross Fixed Capital Formation (GFCF) at Current Prices, 2011–2020*

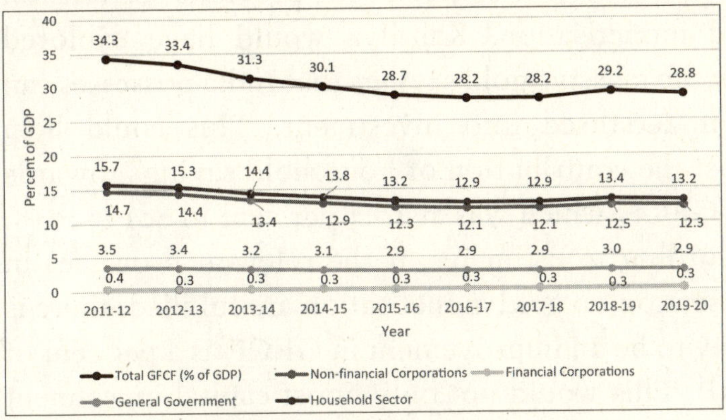

Source: Based on author's analysis of data from *National Account Statistics 2021*

The data shows the decline in the household sector's contribution to GFCF from 15.7 per cent in 2011–2012 to 13.2 per cent in 2019–2020, whereas the non-financial corporations' contribution to GFCF has decreased from 14.7 per cent in 2011–2012 to approximately 12.3 per cent in 2019–2020. These indicate the scope for additional contributions to the investment story in the country through the household sector. It also reinforces the lack of big corporate investment driving the Indian economy, especially in recent times. While greater corporate investment would be welcome, it is important to optimise the huge potential of the household sector in India.

Kautilyan Tantra on Savings, Investment and Growth

Utilising Household Savings Potential to Boost Investment

Managing large gold-related savings

As we articulated earlier in the previous sections on gold monetisation, Kautilya would have explored how the massive gold savings that India possesses can be materialised into investment. This could help boost the contribution of household savings towards the GFCF, which was at 10.3 per cent in 2017–2018. According to estimates, if the relevant processes in the section on gold monetisation are fulfilled, there is likely to be an improvement in GFCF as a per cent of GDP. This would not only boost capital investment but would also boost the overall growth of the country.

> **Kautilyan Tantra**
>
> Kautilya's view on household savings and its importance in enhancing the economy is quite self-evident. He argues that the idea of 'yogakshema', which was central to the Kautilyan worldview—the big-picture perspective—couldn't be built without savings and investment. This would include both the physical assets and the material possessions that citizens possess.
>
> 'That which is the source of wealth is productive ... capable men will certainly secure wealth at least after a hundred trails; and is bound by wealth just as

elephants are bound by counter-elephants' (Shamasastry 1915, 347).

09.4.20 अर्थानुबन्धकत्वाद् वृद्ध्य्।उदयः

09.4.27ab नाधनाः प्राप्नुवन्त्यर्थान्नरा यत्नशतैरपि ।

09.4.27chd अर्थैरर्था प्रबध्यन्ते गजाः प्रजिगजैरिव (इति)

Transition from unsecured debt to secured debt

An interesting example of a good transition from unsecured debt to secured debt is seen in South Africa. As seen in Figure 4.16, the composition of household debt is largely secured debt[9]—which is debt that is accumulated through more robust financial sources. Most of the unsecured debt in India is through ad-hoc personal loan lending through informal transactions. While this is useful for access to instant cash, more sustainable financing can be obtained through more secure funding. Recent trends in the consumer credit industry indicate that the younger generation and non-urban sector have seen a significant increase in unsecured loans. For example, according to a recent study (Goyal 2020), between 2016 and 2018, the number of millennials availing of new credit cards or loans grew by 58 per cent compared to 14 per cent for non-millennials. Kautilya would have reversed this to have greater financial stability. Much of this has to do with the lack of opportunities to gain enough credit in the formal sector. Facilitating this through the digital route can be a good alternative to boost the credit profile

[9] Secured loans are generally considered to be housing and automobile loans whereas personal and credit card–based loans are considered unsecured debt.

and hence can serve as a catalyst towards better-secured debt financing for consumption activities. This, in turn, will have an impact on increased confidence levels among households to consume and will boost consumption in the medium to long run.

Kautilyan Tantra

Kautilya's view on debt security is very balanced. Unlike other historical precedents, Kautilya doesn't view debt-based financing as a taboo. There are many references in the *Arthashastra* that indicate that credit and debt are fundamental drivers of economic prosperity. Hence, he views the need for debt sustainability through the state as a key goal.

Debt sustainability

'The nature of transactions between creditors and debtors, on which the welfare of the kingdom depends, shall always be scrutinized.... An interest of pana and a quarter per month per cent is just five panas per month per cent is commercial interest (vyavahariki). Ten panas per month per cent prevails among forests' (Shamasastry 1915).

03.11.01 सपादपणा धर्म्या मासवृद्धिः पणशतस्य, पञ्चपणा व्यावहारिकी, दशपणा कान्तारगाणां, विंशतिपणा सामुद्राणाम्

Concessional financing and debt relief

'Debts neglected for 10 years, except in the case of minors, aged persons, diseased persons, persons involved in calamities or persons who are sojourning abroad or have fled the country and except tin the need to innovate and keep evolving with the times, would have also expanded the role of digitisation among the masses, given the beneficial impact it has on people. Anything to 'enhance the welfare of the people' was the Kautilyan tantra and one can imagine the usage of digitisation in boosting the SMEs and the smaller investor reverberating in Kautilya's thoughts.

Using Innovative Incentives as a Tool for Boosting Investment

Innovative incentives are an important method to boost the GFCF, which has been declining since 2011–2012 as seen in Figure 4.16. Kautilya also considered the importance of investment albeit in an indirect manner when compared to present times. Since the state's investment initiatives were vested with the monarch and the government, Kautilya tried to use incentives for the private sector to boost investment. They were provided with a variety of incentives for the private sector to invest in the kingdom.

> **Kautilyan Tantra**
>
> Kautilya's view on providing incentives to boost private investment are characterised by quotes such as this:
>
> 'On new settlements, the cultivators shall be granted grains, cattle and money which they can repay at their convenience' (Rangarajan 1992, 179).
>
> 'There have been other instances where certain

> cases of disturbances in the kingdom (rajyabibhrama), shall not be received back' (Shamasastry 1915).
>
> 03.11.13 दशवर्ष उपेक्षितं ऋणं अप्रतिग्राह्यं, अन्यत्र बालवृद्धव्याधितव्यसनिप्रोषितदेशत्यागराज्यविभ्रमेभ्यः

Tax breaks to boost investment

Tax breaks could be an effective tool to boost investment. The inspiration for this, despite recent theories such as the Laffer Curve[10], has been one of Kautilya's according to Sihag (2014) and rightfully so. Kautilya used tax incentives as one of his preferred methods to boost investment.

> **Kautilyan Tantra**
>
> Kautilya's view on using tax incentives to boost investment has been illustrated as follows:
>
> 'In the cases of construction of new works such as tanks, lakes etc, taxes (on lands below such tanks) shall be remitted for 5 years (panchavarshikah pariharah). For repairing neglected or ruined works of similar nature, taxes shall be remitted for 4 years. For improving or extending waterworks, taxes shall

[10] The Laffer Curve is a theory formalised by supply-side economist Arthur Laffer to show the relationship between tax rates and the amount of tax revenue collected by governments. The curve is used to illustrate the argument that sometimes, cutting tax rates can result in increased total tax revenue (https://www.investopedia.com/terms/l/laffercurve.asp#:~:text=The%20Laffer%20Curve%20is%20a,in%20increased%20total%20tax%20revenue).

be remitted for 3 years. In the case of acquiring newly started works by mortgage or purchase, taxes on lands below such works will be remitted for two years' (Shamasastry 1915, 177–178).

03.9.32 पञ्चवर्ष उपरतकर्मणः सेतुबन्धस्य स्वाम्यं लुप्येत, अन्यत्रापद्भ्यः

03.9.33 तटाकसेतुबन्धानां नवप्रवर्तने पाञ्चवर्षिकः परिहारः, भग्न उत्सृष्टानां चातुर्वर्षिकः, समुपारूढानां त्रैवर्षिकः, स्थलस्य द्वैवर्षिकः

This showcases a graded tax-break approach towards investment. These extended to both individual and corporation type of entities. The incentives provided for new construction compared to the repair of infrastructure highlights the level of importance to public services through private entities. Given the nature of population and the quantum of houses being built by individuals, Kautilya preferred a lower concession for buying mortgages compared to public investments. Rightfully so, he was aware that much of the government revenues was also through these taxes and he had to find a balance to boost investment given the fiscal limitations.

Financial Inclusion

The rapid growth of digitisation in India has had substantial successes in establishing a digital identity and optimising non-cash transactions for consumer purchases. More importantly, it has made transactions effortless and seamless irrespective of the nature of the

transaction (consumer or investment). This could provide a valid outlet for consumers to develop credit histories, which wasn't available earlier.

It provides an opportunity to develop a streamlined manner to use the digital transactions of individuals into an aggregated credit history for banks to consider while lending. This accelerates formalisation and provides an avenue for small and medium enterprises (SMEs) to expand with sustainable credit access from the banks. The SME sector contributes about 45 per cent to manufacturing output, more than 40 per cent of exports and over 28 per cent of the GDP while creating employment for about 111 million people. This in terms of volume is only next to the agricultural sector (Sinha 2019). The credit for the sector required is estimated to be ₹37 trillion with the formal credit sources contributing a mere ₹14.5 trillion, leaving a deficit of about ₹20–25 trillion, which is financed through informal sources of credit.

Most of these informal sources of credit charge exorbitant interest rates that make the investment environment very challenging for genuine savers. Hence the transition to formal financing from informal financing is crucial for the savings to investment transmission in the SME sector. The accelerated digitisation of financial services could help to boost the sector through more sustainable financing. The emergence of 'know your customers' (KYC) through digital banking, the Employees Provident Fund Organisation (EPFO) and utility data followed by the vast GST dataset provides ease of loan transactions much more than before. Kautilya, who believed in the

exemptions were provided to the private sector including tax holidays, concessionary loans and also reduction in duties for some goods compared to others' (Sihag 2014).

Similarly, Kautilya would have used innovative incentives to boost investment in the kingdom. While in modern India, there is an additional element of excessive red-tapeism, the need to boost investments through innovative incentives cannot be overstated. The concept of incentives has been pioneered in modern economics as well, through behavioural economics and its newer developments. The Nobel prize-winning economist Richard Thaler, who authored the *Nudge*, was an exponent of innovative incentives for more targeted human interactions on specific topics and ideas as well.

5

Sustainable Growth and Welfare

In the earlier chapter, we discussed in detail the role of investments and savings in pursuing a growth strategy. While the quantum of growth is an important benchmark, the quality of growth becomes even more important. What is sustainable growth? It is pursuing economic growth with the least harmful effects on the environment. Renewable energy, reducing various types of pollution and preserving the natural environment are some of the pillars of sustainable growth. It also helps to address the issue of climate change, which is gaining prominence among policymakers around the world in recent years. This chapter deals with the approaches to sustainable growth in contemporary India and provides a parallel perspective on Kautilya's thinking on growing economic policy sustainably in the long run.

SUSTAINABLE GROWTH THROUGH KAUTILYA

The prism of sustainable growth has various parameters within the main goal of growing yet protecting the environment in the process. While there are many ways to think about this, I look at it from a behavioural lens in this chapter. So, what do I mean by that? Let me explain.

Most people look at outcomes; for example, the amount of pollution reduced rather than the behavioural tendencies that drive the process, such as keeping your own society clean, for instance. The macro-picture is often driven by micro-actions by every individual and their commitment to a sustainable environment. Kautilya looks at this through the prism of responsibilities—familial, societal and environmental—and believes in its aggregation at the macro level.

In this section, we will try to classify recent developments in this prism of responsibilities and provide a perspective on how Kautilya had spoken about them much earlier.

Societal Responsibilities

One of the more important recent initiatives has been the substantial increase in sanitation and toilet coverage in India. The central scheme that has pioneered this has been the Swachh Bharat Abhiyan (SBA) which has focused on cleanliness and universal sanitation as its main goals. The key objectives for the initiative are mentioned on its website:

> To accelerate the efforts to achieve universal sanitation coverage and to put focus on sanitation, the Prime Minister of India had launched the Swachh Bharat Mission on 2nd October 2014. The mission was implemented as nation-wide campaign/Janandolan which aimed at eliminating open defecation in rural

> areas during the period 2014 to 2019 through mass scale behavior change, construction of household-owned and community-owned toilets and establishing mechanisms for monitoring toilet construction and usage.
>
> Under the mission, all villages, Gram Panchayats, Districts, States and Union Territories in India declared themselves 'open-defecation free' (ODF) by 2 October 2019, the 150th birth anniversary of Mahatma Gandhi, by constructing over 100 million toilets in rural India. To ensure that the open defecation free behaviors are sustained, no one is left behind, and that solid and liquid waste management facilities are accessible, the Mission is moving towards the next Phase II of SBMG i.e ODF-Plus. ODF Plus activities under Phase II of Swachh Bharat Mission (Grameen) will reinforce ODF behaviors and focus on providing interventions for the safe management of solid and liquid waste in villages. (Swachh Bharat Abhiyan 2021)

As seen from the details mentioned on its website and reproduced here, the SBA initiative has three components: building toilets, development of defaecation-free villages, and greater cleanliness across cities and rural areas. The impact of the former is much more visible compared to the latter as per the statistics that we will discuss later. Moreover, the impact on rural India is much higher compared to urban India due to a few reasons. This could be because of the greater need for sanitation facilities in rural India and the potential for greater impact through a village-centric approach

Building Toilets and Open-Defaecation-Free Villages

Even though this is a fairly basic necessity, its impact on large sections of the poor has been quite profound. Figure 5.1 shows the increase in toilet coverage over the years.

FIGURE 5.1: *Toilet Construction in India (in Crore), 2014–2021*

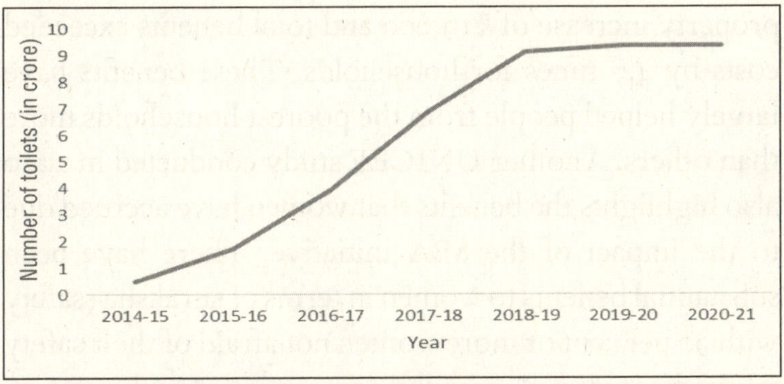

Source: Based on author's analysis of data from Government of India

As seen in Figure 5.1, more than 10 crore toilets have been built since 2014–2015 as per the latest government data. This has increased access to clean sanitation facilities for the poor who had no access to sanitation thus far, especially in rural areas where open defaecation had been a norm in post-Independence India. As an extension of better sanitation facilities, defaecation has become much safer, dignified and environmentally sustainable. The net effect is that this has also led to over 6 lakh open-defecation-free villages [1] as per government data. While there has been some debate on the quantum of complete ODF villages, the big-picture

[1] Latest Swacch Bharat data from the website as of June 2021.

improvement in sanitation across rural India is largely accepted.

Socio-Economic Benefits

According to a UNICEF[2] report (2017), on average, households in ODF villages accrued cumulative benefits of ₹50,000 per year, households with a toilet saw a property increase of ₹19,000 and total benefits exceeded costs by 4.7 times for households. These benefits have largely helped people from the poorest households more than others. Another UNICEF study conducted in 2020 also highlights the benefits that women have accrued due to the impact of the SBA initiative. There have been substantial benefits to women in terms of suraksha (safety with 90 per cent or more women not afraid of their safety while defaecating), suvidha (convenience with over 90 per cent mentioning that they don't need to travel far for sanitation) and swabhimaan (self-respect, with almost 90 per cent saying they are proud to own these toilets).

Clean Water Access

As part of the Jal Jeevan Mission, there has also been an effort to boost access to clean water across the poor areas

[2] UNICEF implemented an independent survey on a sample of 18,376 respondents representing 10,068 rural households, randomly selected from 550 gram panchayats across 12 states accounting for 90 per cent of open defaecation in India. The survey was carried out from 20 July–11 August 2017. This interim report provides an overview of key findings, showing differences between population 'quintiles' reflecting household wealth, based on an asset index.

in the country. While this has been a recent initiative that began in 2019, much progress has been made. The progress of the access of the water is shown below in Figure 5.2.

FIGURE 5.2: *Households with Tap Water (in Crore), 2019–2021*

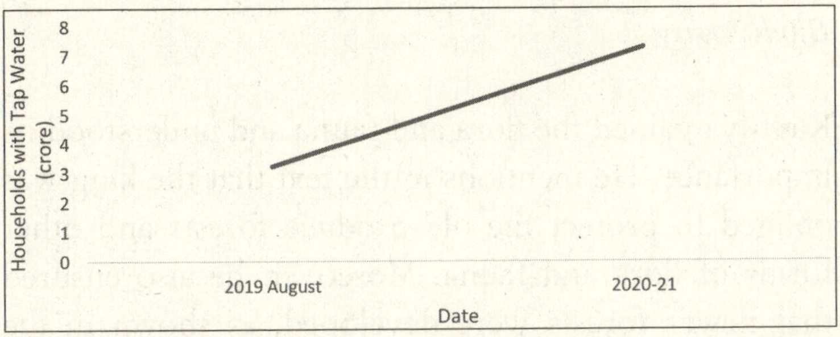

Source: Based on author's analysis of data from Government of India

As shown in Figure 5.2, there has been an increase of almost four crore in the number of households with tap-water connections compared to 2019 as of the latest data. The emphasis on clean water has been another area of focus in recent years.

In essence, the combination of universal sanitation through the provision of toilets in almost all districts in the country, and a focus on cleanliness (including clean water) has been one of the key areas of focus, especially for the rural poor in recent years.

Kautilya's View on Societal Responsibilities

Kautilya believed in the idea of societal responsibilities through the sense of communities and responsibilities. He believed that the maintenance and usage of land was central to the upkeep of societal responsibilities among people. It was a sort of integrated approach of preservation, protection and development of land, forest, animals and vegetation (Sunil 1998). This was achieved through an increased focus on biodiversity, a civic sense towards the environment and animal welfare.

Biodiversity

Kautilya valued the flora and fauna and understood its importance. He mentions in the text that the king was obliged to protect the old-produce forests and other forms of flora and fauna. Moreover, he also ensured that newer forests were developed, as shown in the Kautilyan Factometer that follows.

Kautilyan Factometer

The king is supposed to protect old-produce forests, elephant forests, irrigation works and mines that were made in ancient times and also should start new ones (2.1.39). The irrigation works, by Kautilya's definition, encompassed flower gardens, fruit orchards, vegetable gardens, wet-crop fields and sowing of roots (2.6.5). Forests should be established and due care taken for their upkeep as well as factories for goods need to be started (2.2.5).

02.01.39ab एवं द्रव्यद्विपवनं सेतुबन्धं अथाकरान् ।
02.01.39chd रक्षेत् पूर्वकृतान् राजा नवांश्चाभिप्रवर्तयेत् (इति)
02.6.05 पुष्पफलवाटषण्डकेदारमूलवापाः सेतुः
02.2.05 कुप्यप्रदिष्टानां च द्रव्याणां एक एकशो वनानि निवेशयेत्, द्रव्यवनकर्मान्तान् अटवीश्च द्रव्यवनापाश्रयाः

There were also substantial fines for people who violated the norms pertaining to the environment. More importantly, since Kautilya saw the need for the protection of the environment, it was implemented more rigorously. Kautilya saw that it was necessary to protect biodiversity and also the commercial value derived from it. He felt that the maintenance of these parks and natural diversity has commercial revenue benefits for the state. Therefore, there was inherent commercial value in maintaining these natural resources from that Kautilyan point of view. Another aspect of this dual benefit was also attributed to the civic duties in protecting the environment.

Civic Responsibilities towards the Environment

The idea of civic responsibilities towards the environment wasn't a grandiose plan. It was an aggregation of the impact based on rules that emphasised the need to protect one's community and, consequently, protect the overall environment. In simpler terms, it meant that if everyone protects their own family, then the entire world is also protected collectively.

The idea of behavioural change driving environmental sustenance was also an important pillar. Perhaps Kautilya linked long-term environmental sustainability to two key ideas—behavioural change among the masses and the need to have rules to provide oversight to trigger this behavioural change. An example of it is shown in the Kautilyan Factometer that follows.

Kautilyan Factometer

It is desired that no one should behave in a manner likely to cause any harm to the immediate neighbourhood (3.20.15). To avoid any inconvenience or confrontation, the houses should be constructed in conformity with the demarcated boundaries to be laid with sufficient space between two houses (3.8.3.5); parking space for quadrupeds, fire place, water storage arrangements, grinding mill or corn thrashing devices, etc. should be placed sufficienly away from a neighbouring house (3.8.11); any construction by way of ditch, outside projecting staircase, ladder, water channel, etc. are to be avoided (3.8.21); and for effecting such arrangements house owners, by mutul agreement, may get things done as desired, and should avoid what is undesirable (3.8.18).

03.20.15 सन्दिष्टं अर्थं अप्रयच्छतो, भ्रातृभार्यां हस्तेन लङ्घयतो, रूपाजीवां अन्य उपरुद्धां गच्छतः, परवक्तव्यं पण्यं क्रीणानस्य, समुद्रं गृहं उद्भिन्दतः, सामन्तचत्वारिंशत्कुल्याबाधां आचरतश्चाष्टचत्वारिंशत्पणो दण्डः

03.8.03 कर्णकीलायससम्बन्धोऽनुगृहं सेतुः

03.8.04 यथासेतुभोगं वेश्म कारयेत्

03.8.05 अभूतं वा परकुड्याद् अपक्रम्य द्वावरत्नी त्रिपदीं वा देशबन्धं कारयेत्

03.8.11 एकपदीप्रतिक्रान्तं अरत्निं वा चक्रिचतुष्पदस्थानं अग्निष्ठं उदञ्जरस्थानं रोचनीं कुट्टनीं वा कारयेत्

03.8.21 खातसोपानप्रणालीनिश्रेण्यऽवस्करभागैर्बहिर्बाधायां भोगनिग्रहे च

03.8.18 सम्भूय वा गृहस्वामिनो यथा इष्टं कारयेयुः, अनिष्टं वारयेयुः

The recurring theme among the sutras in the *Arthashastra* is the need for communal togetherness and harmony. The emphasis is always on harmony and coexistence within individual neighbourhoods.

Some of these broad insights from Kautilya have also had similarities with recent international events, including the 1972 Stockholm summit on the environment. Moreover, some of the legislations in India regarding the environment laws—such as The Water (Prevention and Control of Pollution) Act, 1974; The Forest Conservation Act, 1980; and The Wildlife (Protection) Act 1972—have some similarities to the ideas proposed in the *Arthashastra* (Bhattacharya 2014).

Environmental Responsibilities

As mentioned earlier, environmental protection is integral to sustainable growth. In very simplistic terms, the environmental strategy can be broadly segmented into three buckets[3]—the development of renewable energy, the emergence of alternative fuels, and the protection of the natural environment.

Renewable Energy

The graph in Figure 5.3 shows the rise in the role of renewable energy capacity in India over the last few decades. As seen in the graph, compared to the year 2000, there has been a seven-fold increase in renewable

[3] There are many other dimensions to this since it's a vast topic by itself. For the sake of nuance and focus, I have taken the liberty to classify them into these broad categories.

energy capacity in 2020. The increase has been much sharper from 2015 onwards, going from 80,000 MW to almost 1,40,000 MW in 2020.

FIGURE 5.3: *Total Renewable Energy by Capacity in India, 2000–2020*

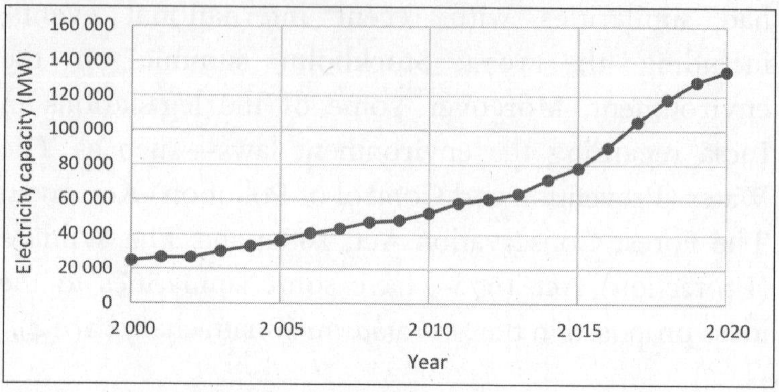

Source: Based on author's analysis of data from World Bank Group

Correspondingly, the sectoral composition of the rise in renewable energy is also interesting to explore. As shown in Figure 5.3, renewable hydropower remains one of the key contributors to the rise in renewable energy. This is despite its decreasing importance since 2010 when solar and wind energy started to gain more traction. In 2020, solar capacity had increased more than 10 times from what it was in 2014. During the same period, wind energy capacity had also increased but at a slower pace. The bio-energy capacity doubled during the same period.

FIGURE 5.4: *Renewable Energy by Source in India, 2000–2020*

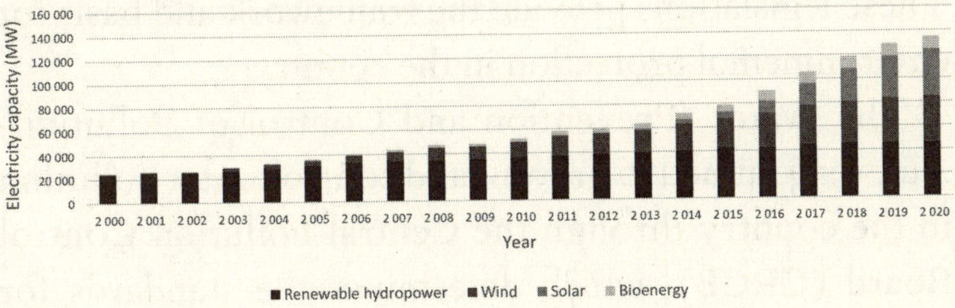

Source: Based on author's analysis of data from World Bank Group

While these have impacted many sectors, one of the biggest changes has been in the transportation sector. The emphasis on electric cars is an important area of development in this regard. There have been new schemes that are aimed at promoting the sector in India. The National Electric Mobility Mission Plan 2020, the Faster Adoption and Manufacturing of Hybrid and Electric Vehicles (FAME) Scheme and the Go Electric campaign are some of the key national initiatives in this regard. There have also been state-wide initiatives by various state/provincial governments to boost electric car manufacturing in their respective states.

Environment Protection

Legislative impetus

Environmental protection has gained traction in recent years with the introduction of various legislations to facilitate the same. These include The Water (Prevention and Control of Pollution) Act, 1974; The Air (Prevention and Control of Pollution) Act, 1981; The Environment Protection Act, 1986; and, more recently, The National Green Tribunal Act, 2010. These legislations provide the framework and basis for environmental protection in the country.

The Water (Prevention and Control of Pollution) Act, 1974, aimed to prevent and control water pollution in the country through the Central Pollution Control Board (CPCB), which determines the standards for the prevention and control of water pollution in the country. At the state level, SPCBs are set up to further the process mentioned earlier in coordination with the central government. The Air (Prevention and Control of Pollution) Act, 1981, provides a similar central board, which provides standards for prevention, control and abatement of air pollution in the country. Similarly, The Environment Protection Act, 1986, was enacted to have standards for the protection of the environment.

The National Environmental Tribunal, established in 2010, serves to enable 'effective and expeditious disposal of cases relating to environmental protection and conservation of forests and other natural resources including enforcement of any legal right relating to the environment and giving relief and compensation for damages to persons and property and matters connected therewith or incidental thereto' (Vinay and Hitender).

Pollution

Despite these legislations, the outcomes have been far from impressive, especially in the major cities. India had six of the top ten polluted cities in the world in 2020 (Broom 2020). Most of this is a combination of vehicle and industrial pollution. Furthermore, the high population density of cities in the country makes the impact far worse.

Kautilya's View on Environmental Responsibilities

Forests

Kautilya makes a clear case of seeing the forests as both a strategic resource and a natural habitat that needs protection. The forests were delineated into various categories with a focus on the preservation of certain types of forests and the corresponding revenue generation for the state. These were pasuvana (पशुवन)[4] (forests of domestic animals such as the cow), mrgavana (मृगवन) (forests of wild animals), dhravayavana (द्रव्यवन) (forests that are of economic value) and hastivana (हस्तिवन) (elephant forests).

Forests as a strategic tool

Elephant forests were one of the more important forests because Kautilya viewed them to be of a strategic and military need on the outskirts of major cities and regions. In alignment with their importance, such forests have a chief elephant forest officer (nagavanadhyaksha), who was trained to protect such elephant forests, in addition to the chief protector of animals (sunadhyaksha). These forests were classified broadly into eight types as shown in Table 5.1.

[4] Some interpretations indicate pasuvana to be forests for wild animals and mrgvana for domesticated animals. This interpretation, in my view, is not appropriate given the Samskritam root 'pasu' refers to cow whereas 'mrg-a' refers to more aggressive animals.

TABLE 5.1: *Elephant Forests and Their Current Locations*

Types of Elephant Forests	*Current Geographical Location*
Pracyavana (प्राच्यवन)	Forests in the eastern region, which is the area between the Brahmaputra river in the east, Allahabad in the west, the Himalayas in the north and the Ganges in the south.
Kalingavana (कलिंगवन)	As the name suggests, this is interpreted as the Kalinga region in the modern-day state of Odisha and the interiors of the Deccan peninsula.
Cedi-Karusavana (कारूषवन)	The forest to the south of Allahabad with the Yamuna river to the left.
Dasarnavana (दशार्णववन)	Dasarna country can be interpreted as being between the Eastern Ghats and the Vindhyas.
Angareyavana (अङ्गारेयवन)	There are various interpretations of this but the most relevant seems to be that of the Anga region in eastern Bihar which is the present-day Bhagalpur region.
Aparanthavana (अपरान्तवन)	The Konkan region in western India.
Saurastravana (सौराष्ट्रवन)	As the name suggests, this is likely to be the forests in the Saurashatra region in the mid-western part of the country.
Panchanadavana (पंचनन्दवन)	The area bound by Kurukshetra to the north of Delhi and the Sindh river.

Source: Based on author's analysis of data from Ghosh Ray 1996

These elephant forests were instrumental to having elephants as a mainstay in the military organisation of the Mauryan dynasty and its corresponding sixteen janapadas. There is also evidence from Greek Emperor Alexander's army and accounts by Megasthenes, which highlight the importance of elephants in warfare.

Forests as economic entities

Preservation of forests also had an economic angle to it. According to the *Arthashastra*, there are a variety of commodities obtained from the forests that are of economic use to the kingdom. These provided revenue to the state and were valuable for the treasury as well. In that sense, it was important that this revenue flow was sustained and therefore, the forests had to be self-sustaining. The key groups of economic products are shown in Table 5.2.

TABLE 5.2: *Types of Commodities and Their Economic Use*

Types of Commodities	*Economic Use*
Plants (vetra, shyamalata) (वेत्र – श्यामलता)	Medicinal and food
Hardwood (saka, arjuna, kusa) (शाक – अर्जुन – कुश)	Furniture for domestic purposes
Bamboo (capa, venu, samsa) (चाप – वेणु – शंश)	Bamboo products
Rope-making materials (munja) (मुञ्ज)	Transportation and other domestic household usages
Flowers (kimsuka, kusumba) (किंशुककुसुम्भ)	Medicinal substances and dyeing materials

Source: Based on author's analysis of data from Ghosh Ray 1996

Other groups of major commodities include timber, wood of other kinds as well as base metals like iron, copper and lead, which played an important role in creating economic activities in the kingdom.

Idea of preservation

Besides the military need to preserve such forests, there was an ideological foresight from Kautilya on the importance of preserving the ecology of forests. The idea of forest preservation, beyond the role of the strategic and economic interests, is seen in the emphasis on forest sanctuaries. These are similar to the heritage sites that we see today in India. His thoughts on the matter succinctly illustrate his approach:

> All types of forests formed by the previous rulers shall be maintained besides forming new ones if need be private parties who come forward to set up a garden, an arched and such may be encouraged with necessary assistance. Forests are to be set apart to yield particular types of produce. (Parida 2009)

These sanctuaries were defined as abhayavana, though there were many sub-classifications on the type of available sanctuaries. This was further extended to highlight the need for reducing deforestation in both commercial and non-commercial activities. Kautilya writes in many places about the need to not burn forests, fields or pastures for clearance purposes. Moreover, there are also fines and taxes in place (dheya and athyaya) for cutting down trees.

Animal welfare

The idea of animal welfare was another important feature of environmental responsibility. Kautilya believed in the need to protect animals through a variety of means, such as better sanctuaries and infrastructure and the rigorous implementation of punishment for violators.

Kautilya highlights a standard list of protected animals. These included boars, deer, cows, tusked animals and animals in crown herds such as horses and elephants (Rangarajan 1992). The village headmen were responsible for preventing cruelty to such animals and protecting stray animals.

TABLE 5.3: *Punishments for Violating Animal Welfare*

Punishments		
For trapping, injuring or killing:		
Protected species	Highest Standard Penalties (SP)	2.26.1
Animals in sanctuaries	Highest SP	2.26.1
For the below offences committed by householders (for personal use), gamekeepers and sanctuary	Middle SP Lowest SP	2.26.1 2.26.6
For trapping, injuring or killing		
Fish and birds whose slaughter is not customary	26 3/4 panas	2.26.2
Deer and animals whose slaughter is not customary	53 1/12 panas	2.26.2
Violations by butchers		
Giving short weight	Eight times the shortage	
Selling bad meat	12 panas	
Killing a calf or cow	50 panas	2.26.11

Punishments		
Injuring animals with a stick etc:		
Small animals	1 to 2 panas	3.19.26.27
Big animals	4 to 8 panas + cost of treatment	
Causing wounds to animals:		
Small animals	1 to 2 panas	3.19.26.27
Big animals	4 to 8 panas + cost of treatment	
Theft of animals:		
Theft of deer or birds held in captitivity for pleasure	200 panas	4.10.5

Source: Rangarajan 1992 and Sihag 2014

Like other Kautilyan ideas, there was strict punishment for people who violated the protection provided to animals by the state. These are shown in Table 5.4.

TABLE 5.4: *Animal Welfare Protection and Their Respective Fines*

Animal Welfare Protection	*Fines*
Trapping or injuring or killing protected species, animals in sanctuaries (2.26.1)	Highest Standard Penalties (SP)
No slaughter of animals in reserved parks (2.26.2)	Highest SP
Protected species include certain types of fish, birds and all auspicious animals (2.26.5)	Middle SP
Injuring animals with a stick for small and large animals (3.19.26, 27)	2–4 panas, 4–8 panas plus the cost of treatment
Theft of deer or birds held in captivity for pleasure	panas
Riding or driving away temple animals	500 panas

Source: Rangarajan 1992 and Sihag 2014

As seen in Table 5.4, there were different sets of fines for different classifications of animal cruelty. These were differentiated based on the rarity of animals (the rarer the animal the higher the fines) and the severity of the violation.

Water management

Water management was also an important area in the Kautilyan governance model. Many dams, reservoirs and water reserves were built during the Mauryan kingdom. Furthermore, there was a thrust to have better irrigation systems that would benefit the masses. This is aligned with India's historical examples of stellar irrigation systems in the Harappan civilisation and others.

Development of Infrastructure

Waterworks such as reservoirs, embankments and even tanks were given priority as prescribed by Kautilya. These were through an array of incentives, private sector participation and accountability through punishments if these waterworks were damaged. They were maintained fairly well, with the state providing grants and incentives for preservation-based infrastructure spending. In simpler terms, the state subsidised and incentivised the building of waterworks infrastructure.

For example, builders were exempted from having to pay water rates—which were taxes—if they were building new tanks and embankments, renovating older waterworks, and maintaining current waterworks facilities for five, four and three years respectively.

These waterworks weren't just the state's domain, they could be privately owned with the private owner allowed complete discretion in case they wanted to sell or mortgage it without any state intervention.

Preservation

Accountability was also part of the preservation ethos since that was important for ensuring the maintenance of these waterworks. Individuals were decreed to pay double the cost of the damage done to a particular tank or embankment that was ordained for water management. There were also fines for failing to maintain the irrigation facilities with individuals needing to pay double the losses for the failure to maintain such facilities.

Taxation was also used to generate the revenue needed for preservation. Similar to how state and central governments in today's India reallocate tax revenue for public development infrastructure, the Kautilyan era had a concept of reallocating tax revenue to preserve waterworks. This was sort of a consumption tax for the people who are using this infrastructure—either built by the king or the natural reservoirs. For example, people had to pay one-fourth of their produce if they had used water from rivers, tanks, etc., for irrigation.

Summary

The summary of the approaches in the current age compared to Kautilya's time is shown in Table 5.5.

TABLE 5.5: *A Summary of the Kautilyan and Current Pillars of Sustainable Growth*

Sustainable Growth Pillars	*Current Status Quo Provided by the State*	*Kautilyan Thinking*
Societal Responsibilities	Toilets Clean Water Swachh Bharat Abhiyan	Biodiversity Civic Responsibilities
Environmental Responsibilities	Renewable Energy Environmental Protection	Forests (economic and strategic entities with preservation) Animal Welfare Water Management
Familial Responsibilities	Swacch Bharat Abhiyan	Personal Hygiene

While one acknowledges the differences in the complexity of today's world, the fundamental thinking during Kautilyan time was not far behind the sustainable energy needs of today. It is evident from this section and the summary table that Kautilya's views and thinking were not far from what we are saying today, especially in the realm of sustainable growth. This reaffirms the fascination with the relevance of Kautilya's thinking in today's time and age.

WELFARE IN INDIA—SOCIAL SECURITY AND INEQUALITY IN INDIA

Social Security through Familial Responsibilities

The idea of welfare in modern societies is largely viewed through the lens of the state. However, in India, the idea of welfare is divided between the state and the society at large. We deal with the role of the state and its corresponding impact on attempting to reduce inequality in the next section. In this section, we will look at how society plays a role of a welfare buffer for much of the population.

Anecdotally, the large size of Indian families and their corresponding savings serve as a buffer for individuals, especially in the informal sector. Even though there is very little academic literature on the subject, the practical manifestation of this is there for everyone to see. The importance of 'cluster networks' or 'communities' among the business class is an important yet largely undiscussed aspect of welfare support for many Indians. An interesting excerpt from Francis Fukuyama further illustrates this unique trend.

> The ability to associate depends, in turn on the degree to which communities share norms and values and are able to subordinate individual interests to those of larger groups. Out of such shared values comes trust and trust as we will see has a large and measurable economic value and trust results in social capital. (Fukuyama 1996)

In India's case, families and kith and kin play a vital clog in the economic social security wheel. While the merits of such a system and its efficiency to serve as a social security net is a different debate, the reality is that society, communities, and the networks associated with them, seem to play an important role in providing a safety net for large sections of the population. For example, if an individual needs financial help, the first person that individual will seek help from is within familiar networks, which starts with family and also extends to the communities around him or her. In most cases, the financing of that individual's needs is met within these contours—meaning, the system of networks serves as financial and social security for that individual rather than the banks as in developed countries. The same happens in the case of social security for the elderly. Since the Indian familial system, even today, is structured in a way that the children take care of their parents and the elderly, physically and financially, a 'social safety' net is in-built into the familial dynamic of the society. The state at best plays the role of facilitator of services and provides an add-on to this in-built social safety net.

The adjustments and provision of liquidity by individual members of the family to others in need within the family serve as the fulcrum of how Indian society has thrived for generations. This is a distinct difference compared to other societies and it would be wise for policymakers to acknowledge this to be able to create more effective policies.

Inequality in India

The focus on growth has been central to the Indian economic story in the last few decades. Rightfully so, given that this growth over the last few decades has helped to bring the maximum number of people out of poverty in Indian history (Ahluwalia 2019). While this is undeniable, as India grows further and existing inequalities increase, the need for assisting individuals who have been left out of the growth story becomes more important. Therefore, the redistribution story in India is likely to accelerate in the years to come as it becomes a more prosperous middle-income country.

In simpler terms, what is inequality? When one is walking through any major city in India, what is the one common feature that we see adjacent to all our modern IT companies? It would be the small shop vendors and slums. Even though the slum dweller and the corporate IT employee live in the same area with similar demographics, their lives are vastly different with a big income gap between these two sets of people. This gap (income, wealth or other forms) between sections of people in a society is broadly defined as inequality. This can be classified in various forms—rural, urban, rural versus urban, the top 1 per cent versus the bottom 10 per cent of the population, and so on—and analysed through various lenses. Several theories are associated with this inequality, some of which we will look at.

Some academics and economists tend to believe that inequality is an inevitable part of a period of fast growth and that growth and poverty reduction should be the top priorities for emerging countries (Bhalla 2003). According to them, this vast increase in wealth due to high growth will eventually lift the individuals who have been left out of the system over the longer run. On the other hand, others argue that excessive inequality can undermine sustained growth and social cohesion (Ostry, Loungani and Berg 2018). This is further attributed to events over the past decade in many countries (USA, France, Chile, Tunisia, Lebanon) that show that people care about excessive inequality in incomes even when average incomes have risen in these countries. This group feels that for a country to grow sustainably, inequality has to be taken care of in the high growth phase rather than assuming growth will take care of everything.

The Level of Inequality in Today's India?

This simple question has a plethora of answers. In this section, we try to examine this through two key metrics—the Gini Index approach and the growth incidence curve (GIC) approach. The Gini coefficient is one of the more popular ways to measure inequality, where the values range between 0 and 1, with 0 being the most equal society and 1 being the most unequal society. The higher the Gini value, the greater the inequality. In India's case, we use consumption data as a proxy for income and compare it with similar consumption Gini in China and Indonesia as shown in Figure 5.5.

FIGURE 5.5: *Consumption Ginis for China, India and Indonesia, 1980–2020*

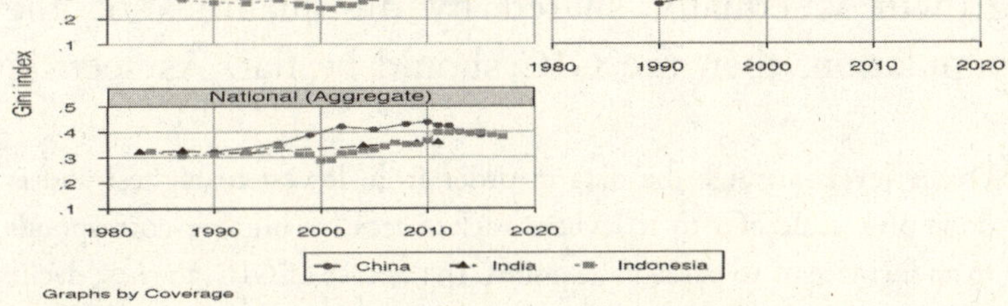

Source: Based on author's analysis of data in World Bank Group

This tells us that the Gini value has been increasing over the years at the national aggregate level, driven largely by urban inequality. Even though rural inequality is also increasing, it is at a much slower pace. We also see that India is more like Indonesia than China, which has seen reduced inequality in the last decade.

The GIC curve is shown in Figure 5.6.[5] For every decile of the population and sub-population (rural and urban), we compute annual consumption growth rates in 2011 PPP in dollars.

FIGURE 5.6: *Growth Incidence Curve (GIC) for India, 1983–2011*

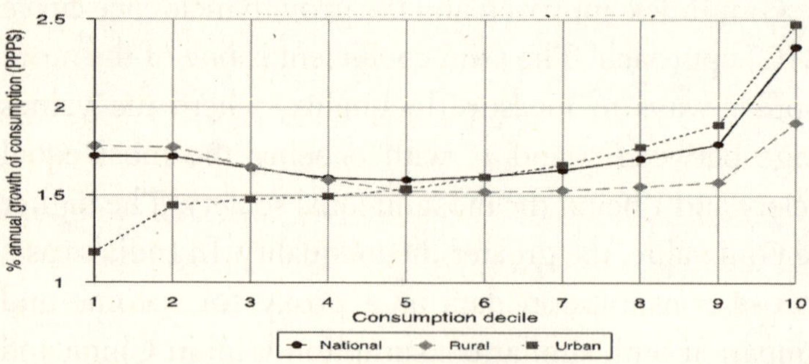

Source: Based on author's analysis of data in World Bank Group

An upward sloping GIC indicates higher growth among relatively richer groups (more unequal). If all growth is equally shared by all quantiles of the population, then the GIC should be flat. As seen in

[5] Decile levels arrange the data in order from lowest to highest and is done on a scale of 1 to 10, where each successive number corresponds to an increase of 10 percentage points. In the case of GIC, the first decile represents the bottom 10 per cent of the population and the 10th decile value represents the top 10 per cent of the population.

Figure 5.6, for the national aggregate, the bottom 10 per cent grew by only 1.7 per cent whereas the top 10 per cent grew by almost 2.3 per cent from 1983 to 2011. Similarly, for the rural areas, the bottom 10 per cent grew by 1.75 per cent whereas the top 10 per cent grew by almost 1.9 per cent. Unsurprisingly, much of the inequality seems to be in the urban areas with the bottom 10 per cent growing by 1.2 per cent and the top 10 per cent by 2.5 per cent (much higher than the rural top 10 per cent).

India's inequality has been broadly increasing over the last few decades and is driven mainly by urban rather than rural inequality.

Steps Taken to Counter Inequality in India

In this decade, there have been a few important initiatives that have transformed the lives of individuals who live below the poverty line. For instance, the provision of the Mahatma Gandhi National Rural Employment Guarantee Scheme (MGNREGS) was initiated in 2006 and has been continuing ever since. One of the key initiatives during this decade has been the Direct Benefit Transfer (DBT) scheme.

The DBT scheme was developed with the main goal of integrating technology with welfare schemes for the needy. It was formally announced as an initiative in 2013 (Narayanan 2013) and has been enhanced over the years through the Jan Dhan Yojana, Aadhaar and Mobile, or the JAM, initiative. As evident in its name, this endeavour aims to integrate the Jan Dhan Yojana, Aadhaar[6] and mobile technology to enhance the efficiency of subsidies transfer. In simpler terms, through JAM, the government aims to send money directly to the bank account of the poorest of the poor who did not have a bank account, an Aadhaar card or a mobile phone earlier. Since they have these things now, the transfer happens effortlessly into their accounts without any middleman involved. This helps to reduce fake accounts and corruption by eliminating the middleman in the system (Kumar 2019).

Previously, when subsidies were provided, we had to go to the ration booth to get provisions such as rice, wheat, etc. In a state like Tamil Nadu, where I come from, these subsidies are provided to all sections of the population. People wait in queues with their ration cards to obtain the necessary items as provided by the government.

So, what was the problem with this? The main challenge was the corruption in the supply chain. When the food is transferred from the Food Corporation of India (FCI)—the government authority that oversees food storage, to the local ration booth—it goes through a variety of middlemen who facilitate the transfer of food. It could be local authorities in the FCI in the state or the local state authorities or even transportation drivers who are involved in either siphoning the subsidies or selling them in the

[6] The Pradhan Mantri Jan Dhan Yogana (PMJY) is a flagship scheme set up to open bank accounts for the poor. Aadhaar is the world's largest biometric exercise which has created more than a billion digital identifications for residents in India. In terms of mobile phones, there are more than 700 million mobile phones in India. The JAM trinity integrates all these three features to enable DBT transfers. Both of these have been integrated with the Pradhan Mantri Jan Dhan Yogana (*India Today* 2019) which has created more than 410 million bank accounts for poor Indians.

black market for higher prices. In essence, what reaches the consumer is much lesser than what was initially allocated. This has been going on for many decades with extensive corruption networks being established. The DBT aims to reduce, if not eliminate, this by providing cash directly to the consumer without any intermediation. The benefit of this is that the subsidies are going to the consumer directly, bypassing all the corruption in the supply chain and the process also liberates the consumer to choose what he wants to do with the subsidy rather than superimposing wheat or rice as a standard.

The DBT initiative has grown substantially over the last few years as shown in Figure 5.7.

FIGURE 5.7: *The Direct Benefit Transfer (DBT) Scheme's Overall Progress Versus Year, 2013–2020/21*

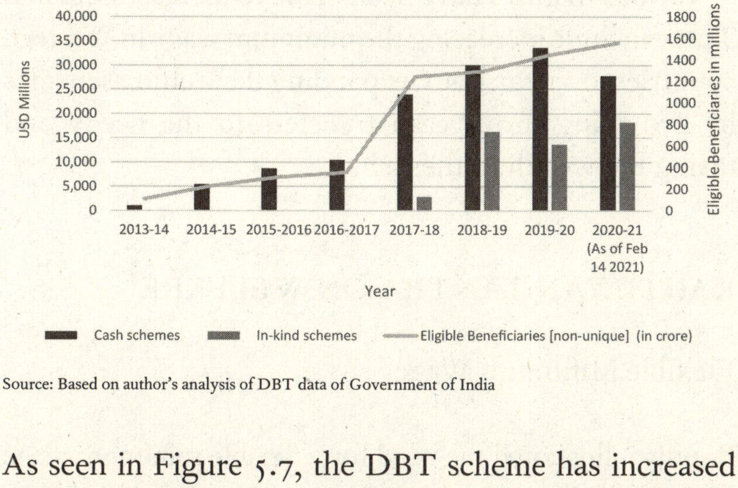

Source: Based on author's analysis of DBT data of Government of India

As seen in Figure 5.7, the DBT scheme has increased from $1.03 billion in 2013–2014 to $33.6 billion in 2018 (approximately 1.1 per cent of India's GDP) followed by approximately $27.7 billion by mid-2020. There has also been a 50 per cent increase in transfers since the data was first shared and, more importantly, this has ensured that during the pandemic, much-needed relief was directly transferred to the people. This seemed to have reiterated the need to refine and expand the DBT system across the board.

So how does this affect inequality?

As the DBT is targeted at the lower decile levels in most states (except for states like Tamil Nadu, which has a universal subsidy system), it boosts household savings and income at the 10th and 20th decile levels (below poverty lines). This enhances the overall quality of life for the people in the lower economic strata of society. Moreover, if the savings from lack of corruption were to be reinvested back into the infrastructure for DBT transfers, there could be substantial improvements in inequality trends, especially if it expanded over the next five or ten years.

Various theories have been made to increase equality. These include increasing the minimum wage in Western countries to $15 an hour, expanding the welfare schemes by providing direct cash transfers to the needy and taxing the wealth of the rich.

KAUTILYAN TANTRA ON WELFARE

Flexible Minimum Wage

Kautilya illustrated the need for a flexible minimum wage for workers in an economy. He mentioned the need for a minimum wage of 1,000 panas for key government servants and had a basic minimum wage of 60 panas for every employee. He also believed in the need for evaluating this value as appropriate. This would imply that he felt the need for a basic minimum wage and that had to be flexible to accommodate the evolution of economic and socio-political circumstances. This is further illustrated in his views on labour contracts where the emphasis on the welfare of the labourer is quite evident.

Kautilyan Tantra

Salaries		
Grade	*Annual Salary (panas)*	*Position*
A (higher grades)	48,000	King's guru, crown prince, king's mother, queen , councillors in civil service, chief of defense (armed forces)
	24,000	Chancellor and treasurer
	12,000	Princes, queens, civil service—ministers, government general of the city, head of manufacturing establishment, provincial governors, governors of fronteir regions
	8,000	Civil service—magistrates, Armed forces—chief commandment of infantry, horses, elephants and chariots
	4,000	Civil service—chief elephant, forester, chief superintendent of productive forests Armed forces—divisional commanders of infantry, horses, elephants and chariots
B (middle grades)	3,000	Palace—grade 1 courtesan

Salaries		
Grade	*Annual Salary (panas)*	*Position*
	2,000	Palace—grade II courtesan, king's charioteer and physician, elephant trainer, chief engineer, animal breeders, etc., Armed forces—camp superintendent
	1,000	Palace—grade III courtesan, soothsayer, astrologer, story tellers, poet, purohitas Civil service—heads of departments, Secret service—intelligence officers, under cover agents
	500	Palace—instrumental musicians and makers Civil service—accountants, clerks, Secret service—village level secret agents Armed forces—commandos and other special soldiers
	250	Palace—actors Civil service—occassional secret service agents
C (lower grades)	120	Palace—artisans and sculptors
	60	Palace—servants in charge of animals and birds, labour foremen, bodyguards of the king, miners, king's other servants

Source: Rangarajan 1992

How is this relevant today?

Much of the literature in the Western world argues for a $15 per hour minimum wage, a demand made especially by left-leaning economists. The minimum wage is not just applicable to developed markets but can apply to emerging markets such as India as well. While other macroeconomic indicators need to be incorporated, there is an argument that this could help us address some of the challenges that migrant labourers and low-wage workers face concerning the amount and consistency of payments. For example, if the local kirana shop employee is assured of a minimum salary per month, this argument suggests that it would be easier for him/her to plan their finances for the year and consume goods as needed. Not only could this add more certainty but it will also give them more confidence to move up the economic ladder. As Kautilya suggested, this wage could be revised in due course depending on the price levels and the economy, thus being a flexible minimum wage for lower-wage workers.

Targeted Welfare for the Poor without Sacrificing Productivity

As mentioned earlier, Kautilya had given supreme importance to sustaining the welfare of the people. The definition of 'welfare' is quite broad but the primary goal is that the quality of life of the people should be of utmost importance. The need to empower impoverished people was one of the areas emphasised. There are many instances where protecting weaker sections of society is highlighted in the text—'priority of an audience with the king' for weaker sections, 'free travel on ferries', 'protection of children from slavery and bonded labor' (Rangarajan 1992, 72). Kautilya viewed this as a way of enhancing welfare for the poor through non-monetary means. On the monetary side, my interpretation is that he would prefer a more targeted money transfer to people than a wholesale transfer to everyone. In simpler terms, Kautilya would have expanded efforts such as DBT to a much larger scale with much greater efficiency for the poor than adopting a Universal Basic Income (UBI), which provides direct financial support to all members of the population over a specific period. For example, ₹1,000 per month for every family in the entire state/country. Kautilya's approach to incentives for lower-wage labourers could highlight this further.

> **Kautilyan Tantra**
>
> 'Kautilya was aware of human tendencies and of risk-aversion and shirking (leisure-seeking). Therefore, middle, and lower grade employees, who might be highly risk averse might seek job tenure. He recommended that this group of employees who were honest, efficient and loyal be made permanent. But he also advocated inspection so that employees did not get slack after getting tenure' (Sihag 2014, 188).

Note the key balance Kautilya makes in providing tenure yet ensuring that individuals are accountable even though they are low-grade workers. In my view, his approach to direct welfare support is akin to this: he would be happy to provide support to the needy (not everyone) yet will ensure that they do not slack off when it comes to productivity because of this. In that sense, the Kautilyan approach would be considered pro-welfare that doesn't hamper productivity.

This is what the DBT aims to achieve. Much of the transfers have been to people below the poverty line and in the 1–2 deciles as shown in Figure 5.6. Kautilya would perhaps make this more efficient and keep it focused only on the 1–2 decile levels of the population. Meanwhile, there could be efforts taken to ensure that the DBT transfers are used effectively by the population rather than being siphoned or wasted. To this extent, it would be valuable to explore how people can effectively use money.

A modern-day Kautilyan approach would be for the government to use these DBT transfers to boost the credit history of the many people who receive this cash. Since most of them do not have a robust credit history, these transactions could help them boost their credit so that they can get financing at affordable rates. That's the reason why it is difficult for the kirana shop owner to get a loan at affordable interest rates compared to a high-income working individual. The building up of credit history from this could be one of the Kautilyan 'nudges' that can help individuals to make productive use of these welfare measures by the government.

Incentives and Protection for Labour

Kautilya believed in the idea of incentives and protection of labour for lower-wage workers and this was also a part of his strategy to address inequality. The dual dynamic served to provide opportunities for needy people through incentives and protecting them from larger-capital owners. In that context, the protection provided through labour contracts serves as an indirect welfare protection measure for labourers. This also highlights Kautilya's attitude and approach to protecting individuals at the lower end of the economic spectrum.

Kautilyan Tantra

Kautilya's view on labour markets and contracts (elaborated in subsequent chapters) is given below: 'The agreement between a laborer and one hiring him must be public. Laborers should be paid wages as agreed upon. If there is no prior agreement, the laborer shall be paid in accordance with the nature of the work and the time spent on it in customary rates' (Sihag 2014, 256).

This also further emphasises the concept of labour rights that he has advocated through the *Arthashastra*. The concept of minimum wage is an offshoot of this worldview.

Kautilya's emphasis on helping the workers without contracts is outlined below:

'Weavers, specializing in weaving any fabrics of flax, dukula, silk yarn, deer wool and fine cotton shall be given gifts of perfumes, flowers and similar presents of encouragement' (Sihag 2014, 189).

02.23.08 क्षौमदुकूलक्रिमितानराङ्कवकार्पाससूत्रवानकर्मान् तांश्च प्रयुञ्जानो

गन्धमाल्यदानैरन्यैश्चाउपग्राहिकैराराधयेत्

Moreover, he also recognised the need to support the lowest-wage workers without any contracts. These are perhaps similar to the 'gig' workers that we are seeing in today's economy—the Uber driver, the Swiggy delivery boy or even the local kirana shop labourer—all of whom don't have a contract or any form of protection in terms of pensions or even insurance. Kautilya felt that such workers should be rewarded on an ad-hoc basis when they put in the extra effort. For example, he wanted to provide additional incentives to workers who fell in these categories to further enhance their productivity as shown in the Kautilyan Tantra.

This has many lessons in the Indian context, especially for our large informal sector. As discussed in the Wealth Creation chapter, this informal sector has barely any form of social or financial protection besides familial support. While this is important, Kautilya would perhaps have thought that it would be also wise for the state to step in by providing additional protection to these labourers without contracts through grants to informal firms or directly to the individual so as to provide extra-reward benefits for productivity. This also leads to the need to enhance the enforcement of labour contracts (and other forms of contracts) for ensuring a more rule-based society according to Kautilya.

6

Rule of Law and Enforcement of Contracts

Kautilya viewed rule of law[1] as an important foundation for economic progress. As highlighted earlier in the components of dharmic capitalism, he was of the view that the state must be rules-based yet unintrusive. So, what is a rule-enforcing yet non-intrusive state? It is focused on implementing the law of the land in the fairest and most time-bound manner while not intruding too much into the lives of individuals through the process. For example, if there was a business dispute between two companies, it would ensure that the legal process is fair and implemented within a particular time but wouldn't impinge on the individual rights of companies in the process of implementing the law.

For Kautilya, the idea of dharmic capitalism would not be fulfilled without a robust rule-enforcement mechanism and enforcement of contracts for businesses. This served as a foundation for the credibility of due process and the business environment. He felt that for international trade and commerce to thrive, stakeholders needed to have confidence in the system and that was

[1] In this chapter, we deal mainly with issues related to business and corporate law. Other forms of legal provisions are deliberately left out since it is beyond the scope of this book.

only possible through a robust rule of law and enforcement of contracts. He viewed this through the prism of 'dandaneeti' and matsya nyaya, which was central to the idea of a prosperous economic model and in turn, would lead to 'yogakshema'.

These two ideas shouldn't be seen in isolation. Kautilya viewed them as by-products of each other. We noticed the idea of matsya nyaya in the 'Sustainable Growth and Welfare' chapter of this book, which was based on the incomes of the poor. In simpler terms, it refers to the small fish getting eaten by the big fish in an uncontrolled environment. In this case, it would mean without the intervention of the state (in general) or, in the context of this chapter, without the regulations to govern the enforcement of contracts. In this chapter, we look at how the idea of matsya nyaya is imposed through the prism of 'dandaneeti', which is the strict enforcement of regulations. Kautilya believed that the latter would be important to ensure that the former is restored in the kingdom.

We will be looking at three key things: (a) Kautilya's philosophy behind rule of law and enforcement of contracts, (b) some of the key trends in enforcement of contracts in the current scenario (the distinction between corporate and sovereign) and (c) how Kautilya's ideas are relevant to these trends.

KAUTILYAN PHILOSOPHY ON RULE OF LAW AND ENFORCEMENT OF CONTRACTS

In this section, we will be looking at both rule of law and enforcement of contracts as distinct entities.

Rule of Law

First, on the legal philosophy, three relevant components of Kautilya's legal philosophy are useful for this book—property laws, labour laws and contractual enforcement. Before we investigate these components, it would help to highlight the role of kingship and people and the relationship between the king and the people in terms of property laws.

> The author of the *Arthashastra* had no illusions about the king's human nature, and seems to have had little time for mysticism, but he recognized the legends about the origin of kingship had propaganda value. In one place, per his quote, he advises that the king's agents should spread the story that, when anarchy prevailed at the dawn of aeon, men elected the mythical first king Manu Vaivasvata to kingship. He thus encourages a contractual theory. (Basham 1959, 83–84)

This reinforces the role of kingship and its impact on property-based laws. The king is viewed as a mere servant of the people—someone who is obligated to protect them in exchange for the rule of the land. In that sense, it isn't the customary kingship that other countries had. In fact, Kautilya goes further to add that the payment of taxes to the state is a sort of salary to the king to protect his people. The glorification of the king is not Kautilya's aim and this strand of thinking is not an aberration by any means.

Across the Arthashashtra, Kautilya makes many references to the kingship being a servant of the people rather than a siloed royalty, as he says:

'A king's happiness "lies in the happiness of his subjects; and his welfare in the welfare of his subjects; a king's welfare consists not in what pleases him but in what pleases his subjects' (1.19.34).

01.19.34ab प्रजासुखे सुखं राज्ञः प्रजानां च हिते हितम् ।
01.19.34chd नात्मप्रियं हितं राज्ञः प्रजानां तु प्रियं हितम्

Other examples illustrate this as well. He mentions that the successor of the king shouldn't always be his kith and kin and should be determined by the potential successor's moral fabric. (The emphasis was on the latter though he wasn't averse to the former having the latter's qualities.) Kautilya goes on to mention that education, moral values and an inherent propensity to serve people were key qualities that were needed for the king's successor. If the progeny were not qualified in these roles, he wanted the most qualified person to take over from the king.

It is in this context that we need to see the relationship between the king and the people vis-à-vis property laws. The king is seen as an equal stakeholder along with the people in the process rather than an uneven player in the field. The main goal is the welfare of the people and the king is a player in that process.

Property Laws and Rights

The property laws were also important during the Kautilyan era. They were three main categories of such rights—common property rights, collective property rights and private property rights (Sihag 2014).

Common property rights

The crux of common property rights is the usage of that particular property. These were properties that were mainly maintained by the state, such as parks or recreation centres, and had a fee for their usage. This fee was used as revenue for the state to further invest in maintaining and developing new public infrastructure. There were exemptions made in some cases (for both humans and animals) for waiving the fee, and that highlighted Kautilya upholding ethical and moral considerations.

Collective property rights

These revolve around the need for residents rather than local authorities in building and maintaining community infrastructure. The rights were designed in a way that would enable collaborative behaviour within communities and therefore, promote social harmony and a sense of collectiveness among communities.

Kautilyan Tantra

Common property

Small animals were charged 1/4th pana, cattles were charged 1/2 pana and buffalos were charged 1 pana for grazing over common property overnight.

Collective property

'Everyone shall contribute his share to the building of common facilities. No one shall prevent the lawful use of such facilities in the neighborhood.... All the people in the village shall contribute their share of the work and the costs of festivals and entertainment' (Sihag 2014).

Private property
'Water works such as reservoirs, embankments and tanks can be privately owned and the owner shall be free to sell or mortgage them' (Sihag 2014).

Private property
Unlike common perception, the role of private enterprise was a well-established phenomenon in Kautilyan times. It is also a classic example of a rules-based yet non-intrusive state. While the common laws of the land applied to the private property owners, they were at liberty to have ownership of the land without governmental interventions in using them. As shown in the Factometer in this section, private owners could sell, mortgage, or use their land as they wished. The de-facto position of private property rights was unconditional since the king didn't have the authority to modify them. However, the king and the state had a right to invoke incentive-based rights on newer settlements. The aim was to further improve the productivity of land use in such instances.

The usage of private property was seen in the development of irrigation in the Kautilyan era. There were 'setubandas', loosely translated as irrigation works, which were both public and private. They were further classified as 'sahodaka setu' and 'aharyodaku setu' with the former referring to wells and tanks and the latter to water in reservoirs by embankments. Private irrigation networks were prominent with specific laws that pertained to them. For example, if private land was not used for a particular period of time, it could be leased or re-mortgaged as per the norm. Moreover, Kautilya also reiterated the protections provided from the encroachment of this property by individuals or the state without due process.

In all these property laws, the exception to the rule was often the role of national security. For reasons of national security, the king could modify some of these to benefit the country at large. However, adequate compensation would be provided to the necessary stakeholders.

Labour Contracts

The labour regulations are an interesting facet of the rule of law and implementation of contractual obligations. At the core of these laws are the employees and not always the employer. In that sense, most of these are focused on the welfare of the people more than anything else.

There is a full chapter in the *Arthashastra* dedicated to labour laws and contracts. They are broadly classified into three main categories—contractual, collective, and casual labour.

Contractual labour

This is illustrated well when Kautilya says, 'The agreement between a laborer and the one hiring him shall be made public. Laborers shall be paid wages that have been agreed upon' (Sihag 2014, 256).

There was an explicit agreement between the employer and employees on the terms of employment. This included wages, modes of employment and tenure. Moreover, unlike in other societies, there was an emphasis on employee rights and not just the employers. Employees had the right to not do the task (even after signing the contract) if they were in distress or were not able to do the task mentioned. There was also a provision for them to transition to a newer job in a more organised manner: 'An employee shall not be obliged, against his will, to continue working for his previous employer if he had completed the task allotted to him and already accepted employment under another' (Sihag 2014).

Moreover, employees could ask for additional pay based on the work they had done. Employers, too, were not left far behind. Kautilya believed in the right of employers to pay the employees only for the time that they worked. While Kautilya addresses the need for a safety net, he seems to have believed in equitable pay from the employers' perspective. Employers were also obligated to agree to the terms of reference with the employee on the work profile and were fined if they didn't. Moreover, additional pay had to be provided to the employee if he or she worked beyond the normal working hours.

If we take a step back and think about this, we will notice many similarities to what we have today. Employment contracts, rights and obligations towards the employees, working within the given time slots

(9 am–5 pm, for example), overtime pay when one works beyond working hours, and the need for the employers to respect the employees at every level.

There were also distinctions between contract, collective and casual labour. The emphasis on the latter two was also substantial.

Collective labour

Collective labour was characterised by rights for the collectives, which would mean unions in modern-day parlance. Employers were fined between 12–24 panas for various violations of the collective labour agreements and the unions served as a collective force to enforce accountability. These could be also in the form of guilds from a corporate point of view, though there is not much evidence in the text to suggest that it was done at a larger scale. However, other Puranic texts detail the role of such guilds extensively.

Casual labour

Kautilya ensured that even the lowest denominator in the labour class, casual labour, was also vested with rights against employers. If employers didn't provide the minimum wage or denied wages to casual labour, there was a fine of 1/10th and 1/5th of wages respectively that had to be paid by the employer.

In retrospect, Kautilya believed in a fair and equitable relationship between the stakeholders in the labour market irrespective of the status of the labourers. Each of the labour categories was addressed and the labour agreements tried to reflect this equity as much as possible during Kautilyan times.

Enforcement

In the preceding paragraphs, we discussed the various legal and contractual prescriptions regarding property and labour laws. While these are good in principle, how were they implemented? What was Kautilya's approach to the implementation of such laws? These questions are important for a few reasons. First, I have often mentioned that Kautilya focused on a rule-based state. A rule-based state is where the laws are implemented fairly and transparently yet non-intrusively. Second, one of the criticisms that Kautilya faced had to do with the strictness in the enforcement of some of these regulations. While they might remain valid from a generalist legal point of view, they aren't as discretionary as they are projected to be from an economic law perspective. The subsequent paragraphs provide further clarity on this.

The general sense that one gets after reading Kautilya's views on enforcement is that of a strict teacher who has a good heart. There were many rules and regulations with numerous fines, which are detailed in nature. These regulations seemed to be intended to ensure that people abided by them. Kautilya believed in the role of dharma and 'satyam' was integral to the dharmic vision of legal enforcement. At a philosophical level, he believed that dharmic principles would serve as a big deterrent to people violating the law. However, he was also a ruthless pragmatist who knew that incentives played an important role in decision-making. As such, he acknowledged that strong punishments were needed to supplement the dharmic upbringing that people had. As a result, he focused on being strict on violations of the law through a variety of fines, indictments and, in some cases, the harshest of penalties (though they were very rare when viewed through an economic lens). On the other hand, he also felt the need to exclude from strict punishment people who were in distress. He was cognizant of the fact that people in distress need some level of exemption from these punishments due to exceptional reasons. This balance between the strict implementation of laws with exemptions for those in distress is a good one-line summary of his approach to enforcement.

Property Law Enforcement

The enforcement of the property laws seems to be based on a set of punishments that are customised to individual activities. As noted by Rangarajan (1992), there were different sets of punishments for immovable, movable and stolen properties. Some of them are highlighted in Table 6.1.

TABLE 6.1: *Punishments for Property Law Violations*

Punishments		
Immovable property	Types of fine	Quotation in text
Tax payer buying property in a tax excempt village or selling or mortagaging to a non-tax payer	Lowest SP	3.10.10.11
Owner of a field neglecting it at the time of sowing	12 panas	3.10.8
Witness providing misleading information on village boundaries	1000 panas	3.9.12
Removing boundaries to hide encroachment	1000 panas	3.9.13

Owner failing to hand over property after sale	200 panas	3.9.9
Obstruction to roads leading to provincial headquarters	1000 pans	4.11.13.14
Tenants who refused to leave when asked to do so	12 panas	
Movable property		
Seller failing to hand over movable property along with immovable property	24 panas	3.9.10
Making false claim of ownership of property	1/5th of value	3.16.18

Source: Rangarajan 1992

Focus on transparency

The key features of this include strict punishment for lack of transparency in information provided. For example, witnesses who would mislead the authorities about the information on boundaries between villages and hide any form of encroachment were fined a large sum of 1,000 panas. Moreover, there was also a similar fine for not reporting a treasure trove. Even in terms of lost property, if someone made a false claim, they needed to pay 1/5th of the property value as a fine. On other hand, the fines were milder in case of activities under individual discretion, such as neglect of fields by the owners. These indicate that honesty and transparency were highly regarded and, more importantly, the opportunity cost—i.e. the cost if one wasn't honest and transparent—was high and the fines were much more stringent.

Gradation based on quantum of impact

There was also a gradation on the level of impact when it came to enforcement. For example, if there was an obstruction to public property that led to any regional headquarters or main roads in the countryside that connected villages, the fine was 1,000 panas. Meanwhile, if there was an obstruction to smaller waterworks or forests, then the fine was 106 panas.

Labour-Based Enforcement

The approach to labour contracts is much more streamlined than others. For example, the fines on casual, contract and collective labour were between 12–24 panas. In a sense, this highlights the importance that Kautilya gave to the lower strata of society—casual labour—over more stable contract-based or collective labour. His view on protecting the marginalised seemed to resonate even within the labour-based enforcement of fines among other things.

These labour-enforcement actions are also slightly different to the ones on property. This difference could be intentional or otherwise since there is no evidence to suggest a priority for either the former or the latter. Moreover, the amount of gradation between the various type of labour contracts is less compared to the types of property laws.

In summary, enforcement of both property and labour contracts is a continuation of Kautilya's philosophy of a rule-based yet non-interventionist state. It is important to understand why he wasn't interventionist in this context. You don't see situations where these regulations superimpose on employees or employers on the type and nature of employment that they need to do. There weren't any regulations regarding how individuals went about organising or using their individual properties. People were given the freedom to do what they liked, in terms of property usage (in the context of property laws) and labour management (in the context of labour laws) as long as it was within the broad parameters of justice. This ensured that the most underprivileged were not taken for a ride, which indicates that the role of matsya nyaya was applied inherently to ensure that the lowest strata of society has their rights vested in the rules. The state intervened only when these regulations were either misused or not fairly implemented. This is an example of the role of a non-intervention state that we highlighted while explaining the conceptual frameworks of dharmic capitalism.

DEBT RESOLUTION AND ENFORCEMENT OF CONTRACTS

Overview of the Insolvency and Bankruptcy Code (IBC)

The Insolvency and Bankruptcy Code has been one of the newer initiatives that have tried to bolster the mechanisms in place for greater enforcement of contracts. As a consequence, it also allows businesses and stakeholders to take risks knowing that such a mechanism could enable them to resuscitate their business after a debt restructured mandate.

The key characteristics of the IBC are:

1. Consolidate and amend laws related to reorganisation and insolvency proceedings for corporate firms and individuals in a time-bound manner.

2. Ensure maximisation of the value of assets to promote entrepreneurship and balance the interests of all stakeholders in the process.
3. The Insolvency and Bankruptcy Board of India (IBBI) will oversee this entire process through other affiliates such as the National Company Law Tribunal (NCLT) among others.

The role of IBBI is elaborated on their website:

> It is a unique regulator that regulates a profession as well as processes. It has regulatory oversight over the Insolvency Professionals, Insolvency Professional Agencies, Insolvency Professional Entities and Information Utilities. It writes and enforces rules for processes, namely, corporate insolvency resolution, corporate liquidation, individual insolvency resolution and individual bankruptcy under the Code. It has recently been tasked to promote the development of, and regulate, the working and practices of, insolvency professionals, insolvency professional agencies and information utilities and other institutions, in furtherance of the purposes of the Code. It has also been designated as the 'Authority' under the Companies (Registered Valuers and Valuation Rules), 2017 for regulation and development of the profession of valuers in the country. (About Us, IBBI)

Let me explain this in simple terms. Assume you are an owner of a large steel manufacturing company. You have been growing the company for many years, and it has provided good profits over the last few decades. For some reason, your recent investments for the business have backfired and the company is making a loss now, and as a result, you have accumulated loads of debt that you are unable to repay. At this point, you need additional support to sustain the firm and its employees; if you don't get it, you might have to shut down the company. In years before the IBC, your company would have been shut down. Now the company can go to IBBI and file for bankruptcy. The IBBI, through the powers of the IBC, will help with getting the company a new buyer in the market through insolvency professionals and facilitate a mutual agreement between the buyer and you. By this process, the company and its debt will be taken over by another buyer who will ensure that the company and its employees stay afloat.

At the risk of being too simplistic, this would also ensure that you would be willing to take business risks in the future, knowing that the IBBI would help to restore the company's fortunes if things don't go according to plan. In that sense, the IBBI provides a risk-taking buffer for companies and entrepreneurs. Such mechanisms are very common in developed countries.

The Status of the IBC

As shown in Figure 6.1, the number of cases referred to the IBC in 2017–2018 was 704 and 1,135 in 2018–2019. This ensured the recovery of almost ₹4,926 crore and ₹70,819 crore during the same periods with a recovery rate of 49.6 per cent and 42.5 per cent respectively.

FIGURE 6.1: *Non-performing Assets Recovered through Various Channels, 2017–19*

	2017-2018	*2018-2019*
IBC Referred Cases	704	1135
Recovered value	14,926 crore	170,819 crore
Recovery Rate	49.6 percent	42.5 percent

Notes: 1. P: Provisional.

2. *: Refers to the amount recovered during the given year, which could be with reference to the cases referred during the given year as well as during the earlier years.

3. DRTs: Debi Recovery Tribunals, SARFAESI Act: The Securitisation and Reconstruction of Financial Assets and Enforcement of Securities Interest Act, 2002.

4. @: Cases admitted by National Company Law Tribunals (NCLTs).

5. Figures relating to IBC for 2017-18 and 2018-19 are calculated by adding quarterly numbers from IBBI newsletters.

Source: Based on author's analysis of data from a Quint article

Subsequently, in 2020, the number of recoveries in IBC totals 45.5 per cent as shown in Figure 6.2.

FIGURE 6.2: *Recoveries from the Insolvency and Bankruptcy Code (IBC) Compared to Other Channels, 2020–2021*

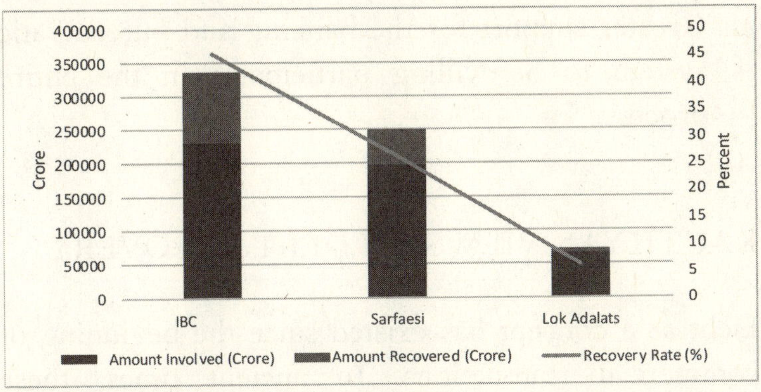

Source: Based on author's analysis of data from a Quint article[2]

It is important to note that the recovery rates for IBC have been much higher than the other methods for similar bankruptcy recoveries. While there are still many challenges in the current system, there has been a steady improvement in the way they are progressing in this regard.

Suggestions to Improve the IBC

Some solutions that are suggested to make the IBC better are:

1. Ensure that the current owners of the respective companies do not regain control of the same companies through other organisations that are indirectly owned by them.

[2] https//www.bloombergquint.com/business/four-years-on-did-rbis-ibc-gamble-with-40-large-defaulters-work

2. Better coordination mechanisms to protect the insolvency resolution professionals (IRPs).
3. Set up more fast-track courts to expedite the process since many of these processes are stuck in a legal quagmire between the Supreme Court and the NCLT.
4. Greater support for the banking and bureaucratic system to be willing participants in the entire process.

KAUTILYAN VIEWS ON DEBT RECOVERY

Debt as a concept has existed since the beginning of commercial transactions. In ancient times, these transactions were made by gold or other forms of assets. There isn't much evidence to suggest that the currencies were rampantly used across the Mauryan empire though there are instances where some form of other proxies for assets existed for transactions. These transactions had both creditors and debtors, and their responsibilities were articulated in a structured manner.

There were two main ways in which debts were conceptualised—through interest rates or a barter system of deposits and pledges.

Interest Rates

The interest rate is the amount a lender charges for the use of assets and is expressed as a percentage of the principal. There seemed to be a mandate in Kautilyan times to ensure there was an agreed-upon interest rate between the debtor and creditor. Subsequently, this interest rate would not be changed during the length of the agreement between the two parties. Recoveries on loans would be made based on this predetermined interest rate. If there was a claim on a loan that wasn't made, there would be punitive action against the individual.

This is very similar to the loans that we receive today. For example, if you go to a bank to get a housing loan, you agree to a particular interest rate, which is followed through the entirety of the loan duration.

Interestingly, there is a distinction in how this interest rate is determined. Kautilya mentions the need to have differentiated interest rates for different types of people based on the circumstances. Of course, in today's times, this is reflected through our credit histories and is based less on the circumstances of purchase:

> The nature of transactions between creditors and debtors, on which the welfare of the kingdom depends, shall always be scrutinized. Interest in grains in seasons of good harvest shall not exceed more than half when valued in money. Interest on stocks/investment (*prakshepa*) shall be 1/2 of profit and be regularly paid as each year expires. If it's allowed to accumulate owing either to the intention or to the absence abroad, amount payable shall be equal to twice the share or principal (*mulyadvigunah*). (Shamasastry 1915, 182)

This shows that an interest was charged on grains and another for investments that were based on the profit margins of individual entities. This idea of mapping the interest rate to profits tended to be towards capital investments that were not liquid. The principle of mapping interest rates to the output seemed to apply to both agricultural output and other forms of investment. Furthermore, the interest charged to individuals who had made sacrifices or were suffering from ailments would not have interest accumulated over a period of time. This differential treatment for people with challenges highlights the differentiated approach to interest payments. The concept of witnesses signing the debt payment to the creditor was also prevalent during those times.

For other forms of debt recovery, some key rules offer an additional perspective on how debt recovery was viewed in those times. Table 6.1 illustrates this in a more detailed manner.

TABLE 6.2: *The Kautilyan Approach to Debt Recovery*

Interest Rates for Debt	*The Kautilyan Approach*
Common interest rate (समानवृद्धि-अर्घ)	1 pana and quarter per month per cent is appropriate
Commercial interest (vyavahariki व्यावहारिकी)	5 panas per month per cent
Interest for forests (वनाय वृद्धिः)	10 panas per month per cent
Interest for traders (व्यापाराय वृद्धिः)	20 panas per month per cent
For people exceeding the above-mentioned interest rates	The debtors would have to pay a subsequent fine as defined by the regulators at that time
Interest rates on grains (धान्य-अर्घ-वृद्धिः)	Shouldn't exceed more than half when valued in money
Interest on stocks (prakshepa प्रक्षेप)	Half of the profit until the end of the loan
Excessive interest payments or claiming interest when not due will lead to fines (अधिकवृद्धये व्ययः)	Fine of four times the amount being claimed

Source: Based on author's analysis of data from Shamasastry 1915

Deposits/Pledges

The deposits/pledges were made by the debtor to the creditor in the form of some asset in exchange for a loan. These were akin to the surety that we use in today's times in the form of a house or some other asset in return for a loan from the creditor. Many provisions are mentioned for these deposits and pledges as shown in Table 6.2.

TABLE 6.3: *The Kautilyan Approach to Deposits*

Deposits	*The Kautilyan Approach*
Pledges (निक्षेपः)	'A pledge, if productive, i.e usufructuary mortgage, shall never be lost to the debtor nor shall any interest on the debt be charged. If unproductive, it may be lost and interest on the debt shall accumulate.' 'When there is any rise in the value of pledge or when its apprehended that it may be depreciated or lost in the future, the pledgee may, with permission from the judges (dharmastanas), or on the evidence furnished by the officer in charge of pledges, sell the pledge either in the presence of the debtor or under the presidency of experts who see whether such apprehension is justified.' 'An immovable property, pledged and enjoyable with or without labor, shall not be caused to deteriorate in value while yielding interest on the money lent, and profit on the expenses incurred in maintaining it.'
Borrowed or hired properties (स्वीकृत-सम्पत्तिःor याचितक-सम्पत्तिः)	'Properties borrowed (yachitakam) and hired (avakritakam) shall be returned as intact as they were when received.'

Deposits	*The Kautilyan Approach*
Retail sale (भागशः विक्रयः)	'Retail dealers, selling the merchandise of others at prices prevailing at particular localities and times shall hand over to the wholesale dealers as much of the sale proceeds and profit as is realized by them.'

Source: Based on author's analysis of data from Shamasastry 1915

KAUTILYA'S VIEW ON THE BANKRUPTCY PROCESS

The implications were straightforward for both the creditors and debtors. Unlike today's times, financial loans weren't complex in Kautilya's era, hence the process of liquidation was also simpler. However, the approach and the overarching principles seem to be similar. Table 6.3 summarises some of the key creditor and debtor implications on debt.

TABLE 6.4: *The Kautilyan Approach to Bankruptcy*

Creditor/ Debtor	*Terms of Debt Recovery*	*The Kautilyan Approach*
Creditor (उत्तमर्णः)	Refusal to receive payment	Leads to a fine of 12 panas. If the reason is relevant, then the amount free from interest shall be kept in safe custody.
	Suing unnecessarily	A fine that is four to four times the unjust amount being litigated. The creditor will pay three-fourth and the debtor, one-fourth.

Creditor/ Debtor	*Terms of Debt Recovery*	*The Kautilyan Approach*
Debtor (ऋणिक:)	Payment of interests	Debtors have to pay the mentioned rates of interest for debt appropriately.
	Multiple debts and their recovery	Debtors cannot be simultaneously sued except in some rare cases. The debtor shall pay off the debts that he/she borrowed in the same sequence in which it was borrowed.
	Debt beyond the person's lifetime	The debt is generally transferred to kith and kin (principle with interest) and there are varied transfers of debt to immediate family members.
	Debt and witnesses	Obligatory to have three witnesses for any debt transaction acceptable to both the debtor and creditor.

Source: Based on author's analysis from various sources, including Shamasastry 1915

Non-performing Agreements

Over and above these fines, the clauses for non-performing agreements were also used. For example, if there was any non-performance between two entities (government, families or even businesses), there were fines in place for the debtors to pay back creditors in addition to their actual agreements. Beyond contractual agreements for work, this was also extended to the debtor-creditor agreements. Many fines were implemented for debtors who didn't follow the contractual obligations. This is similar to the non-performing loans that India was dealing with during much of the last decade.

KAUTILYAN TANTRA ON RULE OF LAW, DEBT AND ENFORCEMENT OF CONTRACTS

The Sama, Dana, Bheda, Danda (SDBD) Principle to Improve the Resolution Process

Given Kautilya's interest in ensuring a friendly business environment, he would have suggested the idea of bringing together all the players and ensuring the process is streamlined. There are a variety of sutras in the *Arthashastra* which allude to the government officials making ease of doing business a priority. This extends to debt resolution and other processes.

> **Kautilyan Tantra**
>
> 'The root of wealth is economic activity and lack of it brings material distress. In the absence of fruitful economic activity, both current prosperity and future growth are in danger of destruction' (1.19.45, 36).
>
> Kautilya's emphasis on the need for 'ease of doing business' was highlighted in the context of agriculture.
>
> 'The king had to ensure that agriculture was protected from harassment by not levying onerous taxes or fines and by not making undue demands for free labour' (2.1.37).
>
> A similar approach is also used for debt resolution.

Furthermore, he believed in the idea of 'sama, dana, bheda, danda' to resolve conflicts between countries. In more simplistic terms, this translates into finding common ground through incentives (sama), providing gifts and other favourable things (dana), finding ways to split the enemy camp (bheda) and eventually forcing a resolution to the conflict (danda).

If we translate this approach to debt resolution, it would loosely be characterised as the sama, dana, bheda, danda (SDBD) approach as explained in Table 6.4.

TABLE 6.5: *The Sama, Dana, Bheda, Danda (SDBD) Approach*

Sama (साम)	Provide incentives for debtors and highlight the mutual benefits of an agreement between the debtors and creditors. In the case of debtors, resolution benefits, and in the case of creditors, benefits of getting back their money in some form.
Dana (दान)	This would be providing incentives for debtors to resolve disputes. While Kautilya characterised this as gifts in geopolitical conflicts, in the case of debt resolution, I think it would be an incentive for debtors to resolve things quickly. For example, this could mean allowing the debtor to retain some parts of the company if he was willing to resolve the other parts with the creditor.
Bheda (भेद)	Unlike geopolitical conflicts, Kautilya's approach would be rather benign here and would involve any legitimate and non-confrontational ways in which the debtors could be convinced of resolving the dispute.
Danda (दण्ड)	As a last pursuit, there would be a need for greater implementation of the rule of law as mentioned earlier. Kautilya would be in favour of resolving the cases through fast-track courts to have better outcomes for all stakeholders.

Protecting the Vulnerable from Being Exploited

Considering the focus on matsya nyaya across the scripture and in this chapter, it wouldn't surprise me if Kautilya had looked at ensuring that the stakeholders such as non-performing loan (NPL) professionals and administrative individuals provided greater legislative and social support in the entire process. Given that big companies might intimidate working-class citizens, it would have been prudent to protect them to ensure greater efficiency in the process.

Kautilyan Tantra

The approach of protecting the vulnerable would have guided Kautilya in the debt-resolution stakeholder system:

'If danda be not employed, it gives rise to the condition of Matsya Nyaya, for in the absence of a chastiser the strong devour the weak,'[3] says Kautilya.

Kautilya also mentioned this in the text in other areas, including resolution of geopolitical conflicts. Given that it has a lot of political value, perhaps the pragmatist in Kautilya would urge him to ensure that the vulnerable are not left out in the process. By definition, the professional enforces and enablers of arbitration—the insolvency professionals (small fish)—shouldn't be eaten (marginalised) by the big corporates (big fish). Hence, the Kautilyan approach

[3] Cited in https://dharmakshethra.com/matsya-nyaya/.

would be to provide protection to the vulnerable and tame the more powerful individuals in the resolution process.

Sequencing Debt Resolution in Different Parts

Kautilya would have also suggested the idea of sequencing the debt owned by the debtor into various components so that there could be a more sequenced resolution of the debt. It would ensure that there was a more gradual resolution, which would provide a buffer to the creditor and debtor to resolve issues related to the money owed in the process. This points towards his pragmatic approach.

Kautilyan Tantra

Kautilya would try to incorporate the logic of sequencing based on the 'dana' principle in the SDBD approach:

'Debtors can't be simultaneously sued except in some rare cases. The debtor shall pay of the debts that he/ she borrowed in the same sequence in which it was borrowed' (Shamasastry 1915).

The idea of sequencing in the quotation seems to be giving incentives for the debtor to resolve the debt with the creditor. It also provides more 'space' for the debtor to find other ways to payback his debt rather than lose everything at the same time. Kautilya would have preferred this approach.

7

How Kautilya Would View the Post-pandemic World

In the earlier chapter, we discussed a variety of current trends in the Indian economy and the Kautilyan perspective on most of those issues. I have tried my best to give a peak into how Kautilya would have approached such challenges from my understanding of his perception of economics and the world at large. However, some recent developments might mystify even Kautilya, especially the impact of the COVID-19 pandemic across the world. My reading of Kautilya thus far hasn't been conclusive enough vis-à-vis such topics, but I thought it might be useful to highlight them to the readers. By this time, the readers might have a better sense of the Kautilyan approach to the economy.

In this chapter, I will highlight key economic trends in the upcoming years and share some questions that one might have asked Kautilya on how he would have approached these issues. Through this process, despite the futuristic nature of the subject, it might give us a better sense of the research that could be done to understand how Kautilya would have responded to the post-pandemic world.

HOW WERE THESE UPCOMING TRENDS SELECTED?

I wanted to approach this question from a long-term macro perspective. The idea was to look at some trends which don't have much precedence in the *Arthashastra* text yet remain relevant to the future of India. These also need to be big-picture ideas that can shape the future of the country in a transformational sense. What do I mean by transformational? For example, if I am to suggest one particular reform or initiative, then its impact will be restricted to a particular area. A transformational idea would be something that has the potential to alter the way the economy and the country function fundamentally and structurally. The economic reforms of 1990 are one such instance since they shifted India from a socialist nation to a capitalistic market-driven nation through structural changes in the way the economy functioned.

In my view, three things will stand out about the Indian economic story in the decades ahead: (a) the changing demographic dividend and its impact on the economy, (b) the emergence of artificial intelligence (AI) and its role in the modern economy and (c) the role of debt sustainability for the sovereign state.

The demographic dividend shift from the world's youngest population to an older one will have a profound impact on how the economic machine is choreographed. We have piggybacked on our demographic dividend for many years, yet some indicators show that in the decades ahead, this trend might be reversing. Much like China and other ageing countries, it will be important for India to understand the gravity of the ageing demographic and develop policies that will suit this given shift. One wonders how we will adapt to such shifts in demography.

Similarly, the increasing importance of AI will have a significant impact on a large country such as India. Given our goals of employing millions, the impact of AI cannot be overstated since it would force us to substantially shift our focus in areas such as skill development and knowledge building. It would also cause us to fundamentally change how we approach all industries, much like how the internet restructured the global economy in innumerable ways. Not only will this alter our approach to things, but it will also redefine the way global dominance will be measured. Data will be supreme and the role of technology in day-to-day activities will exceed our comprehension. In this context, how will we respond to such a technological transformation?

It might be asked why I consider debt sustainability to be an emerging trend. Post the pandemic, I firmly believe that one of the challenges that India could be confronted with is the management of debt for future generations. The pandemic and its impact on the economy has left many emerging markets reeling with a lost decade in sight for some of them. In this context, the support provided by many countries and the amount of debt overload could be an important trend to look at. I try to provide a history of how India's debt position has evolved and what could be some of the challenges in the decades ahead. The need to understand and navigate this might be one of the defining trends in the years to come. One also wonders how AI and demography will affect our debt sustainability, among other things.

I wonder how Kautilya would have responded and how he would have approached these challenges. I don't offer any big solutions here since I am also in the process of pondering these trends and their impact. However, if Kautilya had been in front of me today, there are some questions I would have liked to ask him, which is what I am putting forth in the following paragraphs. Perhaps, this will also help to get answers from readers on what they think Kautilya's perspective on these issues would have been. Or even how Kautilya would have responded to such socio-economic trends.

Demographics in a Post-pandemic World

One of the important trends that India will have to confront in the decades ahead is the demographic challenge. While much of the discourse has been centred on the demographic dividend that India has, which refers to having one of the world's youngest populations, one of the important trends in the decades ahead is the number of elderly the country will possess. This might not be of immediate concern but economic policy certainly needs to be shaped to address this.

According to population estimates, India is expected to have the largest number of senior citizens after China in a few decades. The most important dynamic that one needs to be aware of is the overall dependency on the government to address these challenges. The graph from the Economic Survey of India in Figure 7.1 illustrates the reduction in the growth rate of the population compared to the previous decades.

FIGURE 7.1: *Population Growth Rate, 1940–2016*

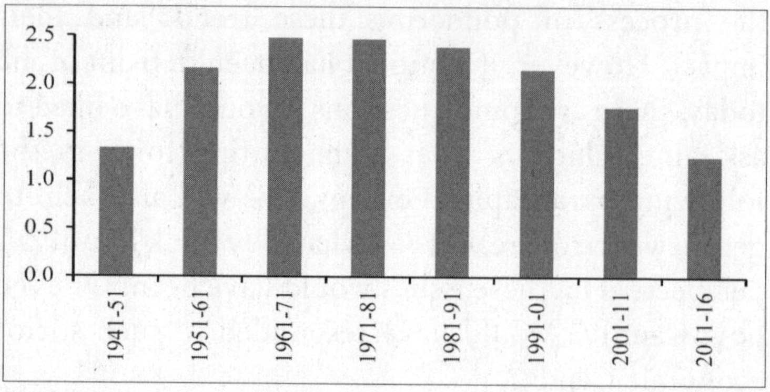

Source: Based on author's analysis of data from *Economic Survey*, Ministry of Finance, Government of India

While this has been an important policy goal ever since Independence, the fact of the matter is that in the next few decades, this might also pose a different demographic challenge that the country needs to address. The total fertility rate (TFR), which helps to measure the total number of children born or likely to be born to a woman of child-bearing age in her lifetime, has reached the threshold of 2.1 in many of the Indian states. Some states have already gone much below the threshold as shown in Figure 7.2.

FIGURE 7.2: *Replacement Fertility Levels across Indian States*

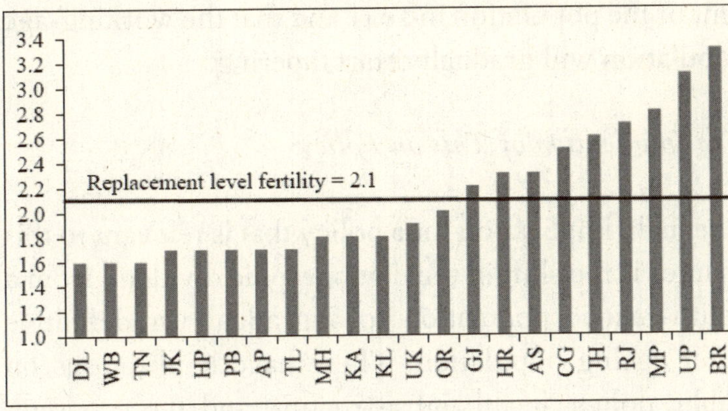

Source: Based on author's analysis of data from *Economic Survey*, Ministry of Finance, Government of India

It is also expected by the forecast in the Economic Survey of India that the country will reach 1.8 by 2021 itself and the overall country's TFR for 2031 and 2041 are 1.7 and 1.7 respectively. This shows a consistent decline in TFR over the medium and longer-term.

As a consequence, there is a natural tendency that a lesser number of children being born would mean a lower percentage of youth in the population. Given the increase in life expectancy of the populace for the senior citizens, they are expected to live longer and have a larger share of the overall population in the years ahead. Table 7.1 further illustrates this trend.

TABLE 7.1: *The Percentage of Elderly in India, 2011–2041*

	0–19 years				20–59 years				60 years and above			
States	2011	2021	2031	2041	2011	2021	2031	2041	2011	2021	2031	2041
India	40.9	34.5	28.8	25.2	50.5	55.8	58.8	58.9	8.6	9.7	12.4	15.9

Source: Based on author's analysis of data from *Economic Surveys*, Ministry of Finance, Government of India'

This shows that people above 60 years will be 15.9 per cent of the population in 2041 and that the working-age population will gradually start tapering.

The Implication of This on Policy

The main implication for a policy that is relevant to this chapter is the shift in the demographic dividend from a youth-centric population to a gradual yet definitive older ageing population. These have implications on public policy, health infrastructure and the economy and society at large. A balance is needed to ensure a population that is reasonably growing doesn't become a liability for the prosperity of the country. In that sense, if these levels keep going lower, systems need to be in place for the older population to be taken care of. Many countries such as Japan have catered to this need systematically.

Questions for Kautilya

1. How does one approach the issue of an ageing population?
2. Does one optimise the present, which would mean making the most use of the young population to grow the country, or think about investing in the future right away?
3. What are the policy implications for the changes in the demographic dividend?

4. How does the country maintain a balance between both ends of the population debate?

Artificial Intelligence in a Post-pandemic World

AI is a buzzword that has been used many times in futuristic policy discussions. The world in the next few decades will be determined by how countries react to the developments in AI. It has been the central debate around employment, technology and its global interfaces. In a country with a large informal sector population, the premium on job creation becomes even more important. While many view AI and its technological advancements as the wonder of our times, one needs to get a perspective on the impact that it has on the common populace. Some common questions include:

1. What is the level of adaptation required?
2. How will the demographic changes matter in an AI-centric world?
3. What is the level of skill development that is needed?
4. Which are the sectors that could be impacted the most due to AI?
5. What are the strategies and solutions to deal with AI?

While all of these questions are important, the most relevant one to us is the last one, which is about finding solutions to deal with AI. This is an important question that policymakers will have to address. In a recent report by NITI Aayog (2018), the government's premier economic think tank, five key areas have been highlighted as core areas for AI in India.

1. Increased access and affordability of quality healthcare
2. Enhanced farmers' income, increased farm productivity and reduction of wastage
3. Improved access and quality of education
4. Smart cities and infrastructure efficiency and connectivity for the burgeoning urban population
5. Smarter and safer modes of transportation and improving traffic and congestion problems

The report predicts that these areas are likely to be fundamentally transformed with the advent of AI. Since they are integral to the broader economy, the impact is significant among main stakeholders. The report goes on to highlight the key areas that are lacking in the AI ecosystem:

1. Lack of broad-based expertise in research and application of AI.
2. Absence of enabling data ecosystems—access to intelligent data.
3. High resource cost and low awareness for adoption of AI.
4. Privacy and security, including a lack of formal regulations around anonymisation of data.
5. Absence of collaborative approach to adoption and application of AI.

The plethora of areas associated with AI need to be studied for a way forward. This is an area where most policymakers are hedging their bets on the most viable options, with no one knowing how it will evolve in the years ahead. In such instances, some prefer to plan meticulously with various options whereas others, especially those who believe in complexity economics[1], tend to focus on adaptability while responding to such futuristic events. This is eloquently described in the lecture given by Nobel prize–winner Fredrick Von Hayek when he accepted his prize.

> This brings me to the crucial issue. Unlike the position that exists in the physical sciences, in economics and other disciplines that deal with essentially complex phenomena, the aspects of the events to be accounted for about which we can get quantitative data are necessarily limited and may not include the important ones. While in the physical sciences it is generally assumed, probably with good reason, that any important factor which determines the observed events will itself be directly observable and measurable; in the study of such complex phenomena as the market, which depend on the actions of many individuals, all the circumstances which will determine the outcome of a process, for reasons which I shall explain later, will hardly ever be fully known or measurable. And while in the physical sciences the investigator will be able to measure what on the basis of a prima facie theory he

[1] In very simple terms, the approach states that complexities are bound to happen in the world. As such, more than predicting these complexities, adapting to them with the most balanced approach possible without too much reliance on theoretical forecasting models is the way forward for any given situation.

> thinks important, in the social sciences, often that is treated as important which happens to be accessible to measurement. This is sometimes carried to the point where it is demanded that our theories must be formulated in such terms that they refer only to measurable magnitudes. (Von Hayek 1974)

In my view, this approach is more relevant to an unknown entity such as AI rather than predictive models and trends. Kautilya's thinking needs to be positioned in this context of different approaches to dealing with AI. I wonder what some of the Kautilyan attributes are that can be applied to approach this situation. The following box highlights some prospective questions for Kautilya that could provide us with more answers.

Questions for Kautilya

1. How does one philosophically approach the issue of AI through the complexity economic approach or a straightforward planning ahead approach?
2. Given the ubiquitous nature of AI, what should the contours of AI regulation be? Should it be non-intrusive or should it be handheld by the state?
3. What about the political economy impacts of AI? How does one cope with the employment deficit cause by AI given that many jobs will be lost with

its development? How should re-skilling be approached?

4. How does one enforce the idea of matsya nyaya in terms of the centralisation of data power in big AI companies?
5. How does one leverage all the benefits from AI?

Debt Sustainability in a Post-pandemic World[2]

Background

The concept of government debt is an important one, given its role in financing public expenditure. Most governments have historically borrowed to finance additional spending, whether on wars, or public development projects. These borrowings are largely financed by those with surplus funds, that is, funds that are left over after spending on their consumption (savings). These savings may be domestic, external or a combination of both.

The composition of debt is largely an outcome of policy preferences of domestic policymakers as some countries are more open to borrowing through external sources while countries such as India have the bulk of their outstanding debt in the form of domestic borrowings.

An important role of public expenditure is to correct market failures and to make provisions for public goods

[2] The following section has been co-authored with Karan Bhasin, who is an independent economist.

wherever necessary. An additional role it has is to serve as a stabilising policy in the event of a sharp economic downturn. Thus, during normal times, fiscal policy must be modest while it must be proactively used in the event of a crisis. It is in this context that one needs to view the COVID-19 pandemic's impact on India's debt sustainability parameters. Countries such as India have provided financial support to their citizens through a variety of means:

> India's central government fiscal support measures can be divided into two broad categories (i) above-the-line measures which include government spending (about 3.5 per cent of GDP, of which about 2.2 per cent of GDP is estimated to have been utilized in the past fiscal year), foregone or deferred revenues (about 0.3 per cent of GDP falling due within the past fiscal year) and expedited spending (about 0.3 per cent of GDP falling due within the past fiscal year); and (ii) below-the-line measures designed to support businesses and shore up credit provision to several sectors (about 5.3 per cent of GDP). (IMF 2021)

In simpler terms, direct government spending through cash transfers and other forms of government spending was about 3.5 per cent of the GDP. The other forms of support—through concessional loans for small businesses, support for sectors that have been affected by the pandemic and relaxing of norms so that businesses get some breathing space, among other things—were expected to be about 5.3 per cent of the GDP. So how does the government obtain money to make these support initiatives; in other words, how does it finance this government expenditure?

Governments may either finance it by debt or by tax revenues and hence the deployment of funds becomes important. That is, a fiscal policy largely financed by debt, which creates long-term assets, is better compared to one where it is used to meet revenue expenditures. That is, creating productive assets that augment growth in the future is preferred as they result in higher tax revenues, which enables the government to meet debt obligations over a longer period. Therefore, the *composition* of the expenditure profile matters.

In the context of India, there have been periods of high fiscal deficits. The best example was in the 1980s, which resulted in the 1991 balance of payment (BOP) crisis. A key point about India's sovereign debt profile is that it is largely owned by domestic players. Thus, the key constraint on India's borrowing programmes is largely the level of domestic savings, the balance of payment consideration and potential inflationary risks. The high fiscal deficits during the late 2000s and early 2010s resulted in inflation and the taper tantrum[3] episode.

However, for a complete discussion on deficits, one has to look at the evolution of India's growth along with the deficits. India's post-Independence economic performance during the first three decades

[3] The phrase 'taper tantrum' describes the 2013 surge in US Treasury yields, resulting from the Federal Reserve's (Fed) announcement of future tapering of its policy of quantitative easing. For more information, visit https://www.investopedia.com/terms/t/taper-tantrum.asp

was termed the Hindu rate of growth by late Raj Krishna of the Delhi School of Economics. However, the Indian economy departed this Hindu rate of growth in the 1980s and 1990s and ever since then, the economy has managed to grow beyond the 3 per cent rate of growth.

After the 1991 reforms, it was expected that India's growth would accelerate further but to the surprise of many, it stayed consistent with the average growth rate that was achieved during the 1980s. As illustrated earlier, one of the major reasons behind the high growth rate during the 1980s has been the build-up of external debt, which wasn't sustainable. Thiruvadanthai, for instance, finds that a major part of the high growth rate during the 1980s could be explained by the high fiscal deficit. While he has no evidence to suggest that the 1991 balance of payment (BOP) crisis was because of the high fiscal deficit, other authors believe that the high fiscal deficit led to the BOP crisis. They further argue that the growth during the 1990s came with the backdrop of external stability and despite the East Asian crisis (Kohli 2006, Srinivasan and Tendulkar 2003, Ahluwalia 2002) which suggests that growth in the 1990s was largely sustainable.

It is therefore evident that while debt is important for augmenting public goods and alleviating the potential growth rate of an economy, excessive borrowing comes with risks.

The following section will provide a perspective on how this government expenditure can be financed and, more importantly, the historical trends regarding debt in India including a discussion on the 1991 economic crisis. We also look at such trends (on debt, deficits and reserves) from a global perspective and compare them with other emerging market economies. Post this, we evaluate the costs of government borrowings and explore outstanding debt and its relationship with a risk premium. This is important for readers to understand since the issue of debt created by the pandemic is likely to be an important factor in the decades ahead. In that sense, a historical perspective is important to show the reader how India has dealt with this issue in the recent past. Furthermore, the following section will also have a box item on some questions for Kautilya that future research can focus upon.

India's Debt Profile Composition over the Years

The debt profile of any country depends on a variety of factors, the most important of which is the policy preferences of the country. Given that public borrowings are financed by domestic savings—monetisation—or future taxes, the extent of domestic savings serves as a constraint on the public borrowing programme. Thus, the public borrowing programme is a function of domestic savings and policy preferences to allow for external sovereign borrowings.

In terms of external borrowings, it is important to distinguish between two different kinds of borrowings. The first is the debt denominated in the domestic currency while the second pertains to debt denominated in external currencies such as the Euro, the US dollar and so on. The decision for the denomination of currency is again contingent on the risk preference of the policymakers.

India's debt profile has evolved considerably over the decades. It is important to note that, since 1991, the composition of external debt has reduced significantly. This is partly due to heightened risk aversion because of BOP constraints. Incidentally, India's policymakers are risk-averse and tend to refrain from issuing debt in foreign denominated currencies. Figure 7.3 shows the Indian government's share of external and internal liabilities. Over the last several years, the share of internal liabilities has increased substantially, and the external borrowings have a share close to 5 per cent.

High public borrowings during the 1980s led to significantly higher fiscal and current account deficits. Consequently, in 1991, there were limited foreign reserves available to meet the import bill of the economy and the country undertook a loan from the IMF and attempted to reform the economy. The reforms were geared towards having a more open economic system, undertaking delicensing, limiting the control of the state over economic activity and having a more flexible or appropriate exchange rate regime. That the country witnessed a significant constraint on its ability to generate foreign reserves was an important feature in the policy decision to avoid foreign-denominated sovereign debt in India. It is equally important to note that there is a material reduction in the share of India's external liabilities post the sovereign debt crisis in East Asian countries, which further strengthened the trend to depend extensively on domestic borrowings.

FIGURE 7.3: *The Composition of India's Public Borrowing Programme*

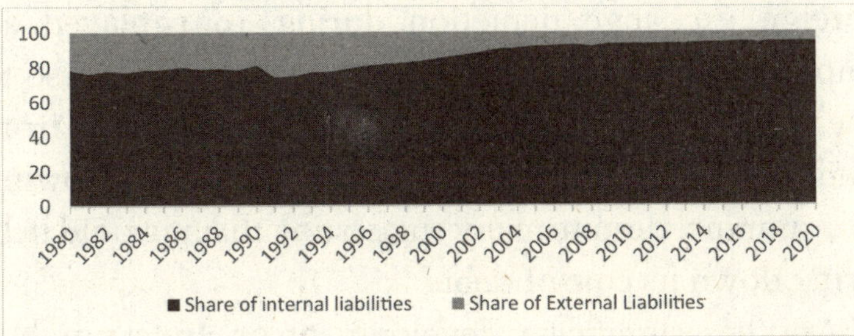

Source: Based on author's analysis of data from *Handbook of Statistics on the Indian Economy*, RBI

When it comes to public debt, it is viewed against GDP rather than in terms of an absolute metric. Debt as a percentage of GDP provides us with an important metric of the total outstanding liabilities against the size of the overall economy. Figure 7.4 captures the debt as a percentage of GDP for India's domestic and external liabilities. We find a similar trend here as India's external debt as a percentage of GDP has reduced substantially—and there is a significant reduction that started post the 1991 crisis.

FIGURE 7.4: *Debt as a Percentage of GDP, 1982–2019*

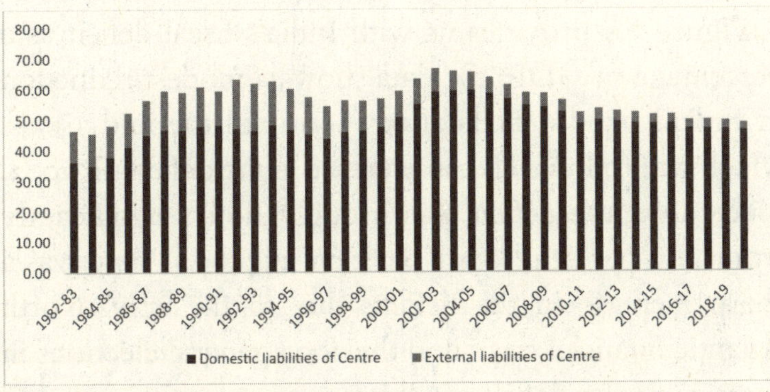

Source: Based on author's analysis of data from *Handbook of Statistics on the Indian Economy*, RBI

India's severe constraints in terms of dealing with the foreign exchange depletion during 1991 played an important role in making policymakers risk-averse to the point that the government has so far refrained from undertaking a comprehensive sovereign borrowing programme, despite many suggesting that it would help bring down its cost of debt.

Another significant development on India's public finance front has been the adoption of the Fiscal Responsibility and the Budget Management (FRBM) Act, 2003. The act was introduced to reduce India's deficit and debt as a percentage of GDP and to follow long-term prudent macroeconomic policies. There are two measures to evaluate the impact of the FRBM Act on the government borrowing programme. The first is debt as a percentage of GDP, and we can see from Figure 7.4 that the total liabilities as a percentage of GDP have indeed consistently reduced since 2003. A major reason behind this could be the acceleration in growth rates and the size of the economy. A reduction in fiscal deficit has also played an important role in terms of adding fewer public liabilities to the numerator.

Figure 7.5 provides us with India's fiscal deficit as a percentage of GDP; the data shows a modest reduction in India's fiscal deficits after 1990 until the mid-1990s, which was followed by an increase in the deficit till 2003. Since 2003 the deficit was brought down significantly from 11.2 per cent to 4.5 per cent in 2007. There was a sharp increase in the deficits due to the 2008 North Atlantic financial crisis and the 2009 general elections in India with the deficit touching 9 per cent in 2008 and 2009, after which it has tended to reduce. However, there has been a sharp uptick in India's fiscal deficit in 2020 and 2021 as an outcome of the growth slowdown that India has experienced since 2019 and because of the COVID-19 pandemic, which necessitated a strong fiscal response from the government to cushion the economy from the impact of one of the world's strongest lockdowns.

FIGURE 7.5: *India's Fiscal Deficit as a Percentage of GDP, 1990–2024*

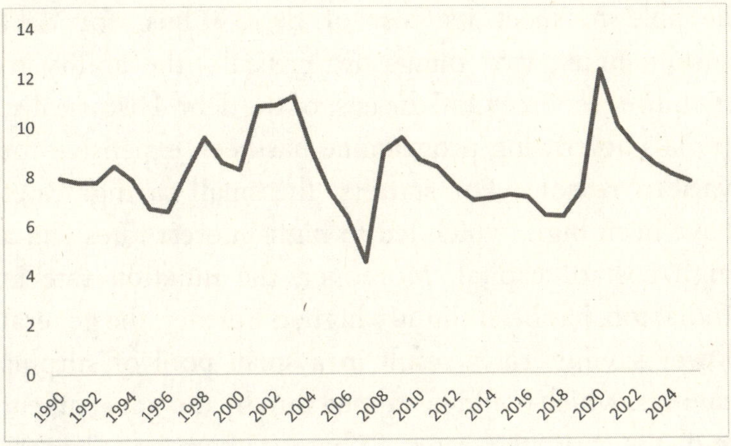

Source: Based on author's analysis of data from *International Financial Statistics*, IMF

The IMF projects India's fiscal deficit to gradually reduce over the coming years, given that the bulk of the fiscal response was a one-time transfer and that the economy is likely to recover and grow faster over the coming years. Therefore, the fiscal deficit is expected to reduce from 12.25 per cent to 7.7 per cent in 2025 as per the IMF projections.

Cost of Borrowings and Debt Sustainability

Most of the discussion on public debt has focused on cautioning politicians, policymakers and other government representatives about the consequences of excessive debt. This discussion has looked at evaluating the optimal percentage of public debt in an economy, ensuring the sustainability of public borrowing programmes and prescribing threshold limits to avoid any macroeconomic imbalances.

Many have expressed concerns about the Indian government's ability to generate adequate resources to be able to meet its cost of debt. Thus, for debt sustainability, two things are critical—the ability to mobilise resources and the cost of the debt. Historically, India's borrowing programme has been expensive for various reasons. For starters, the small savings rates have been high, which led to high-interest rates and a high cost of capital. Moreover, the inflation rate in India, too, has been slightly higher. Further, the general lower savings rates result in a small pool of surplus savings, which could be tapped into by the government and the private sector. These factors are largely responsible for the overall high costs associated with India's borrowing programme.

Table 7.2 captures the total central government debt that is due to mature between 2020–2024 along with the weighted average cost of the debt. As evident, the cost is substantially higher and well above 7.5 per cent (approximately 7.7 per cent on average). To give some context, the fresh borrowing programme post the pandemic has seen the RBI attempt to contain the yields to 6 per cent. Thus, the existing debt is substantially higher compared to the costs associated with the current borrowings. One reason behind the low cost of fresh borrowings is the general moderation in inflation levels and the excessive monetary easing by the RBI in response to the pandemic.

TABLE 7.2: *Central Government Borrowings, 2020–2024*

Year	Total Debt Maturing (in ₹, in crore)	Weighted Average Cost of Debt
2020	4,26,545.96	7.74
2021	2,29,130.98	8.46
2022	4,67,097.02	7.84
2023	3,16,526.04	7.67
2024	3,93,133.05	7.72

Source: Based on author's analysis of data from Department of Economic Affairs, Government of India

Given India's infrastructural gap, there is a need for sizeable public investments in the area, and a low-cost government borrowing programme can help accelerate these investments, thereby creating fresh capacity in the overall economy. Table 7.3 provides a comprehensive list of the existing securities along with the coupon rate[4] and the total outstanding stock. Several securities attract a coupon rate above 8 per cent while some even attract 10 per cent or 11 per cent. In terms of ensuring the sustainability of debt and in the interest of bringing the costs of borrowing down, some of the high-cost government bonds could be replaced with fresh borrowings at a lower cost. The RBI undertakes similar

[4] Coupon rate is the rate of interest paid by bond issuers on the bond's face value. It is the periodic rate of interest paid by bond issuers to its purchasers. For example, if you have a 10-year ₹1,000 bond with a coupon rate of 10%, you will get ₹100 every year for 10 years, no matter what happens to the bond price in the market.

exercises and terms them as 'switches', which helps in bringing down the cost of borrowings.

However, a debt management office in the Department of Economic Affairs would help to better plan the government borrowing programme in coordination with the RBI. Further, it will help in better management of the costs of the government borrowing programme as it can regularly tweak India's debt composition with the interest of reducing the annual expenditure on debt servicing.

TABLE 7.3: *List of Outstanding Government Securities*

Nomenclature	*Coupon (%)*	*Date of First Issue*	*Date of Maturity*	*Outstanding Stock (in ₹, in crore)*
6.35 per cent Government Securities (GS) 2020 (convertible)	6.35	2 January 2003	2 January 2020	61,000
8.19 per cent GS 2020	8.19	16January 2012	16 January 2020	74,000
6.65 per cent GS 2020	6.65	9 April 2018	9 April 2020	43,545.96
10.70 per cent GS 2020	10.7	22April 2000	22 April 2020	6,000
7.80 per cent GS 2020	7.8	3 May 2010	3 May 2020	75,000
8.27 per cent GS 2020	8.27	9 Jun e2014	9 June 2020	73,000
8.12 per cent GS 2020	8.12	10 December 2012	10 December 2020	76,000
6.87 per cent GS 2020	6.87	21 December 2009	21 December 2020	13,000

Nomenclature	*Coupon (%)*	*Date of First Issue*	*Date of Maturity*	*Outstanding Stock (in ₹, in crore)*
11.60 per cent GS 2020	11.6	27 December 2000	27 December 2020	5,000
7.00 per cent GS 2021	7	21 January 2019	21 January 2021	3,000
7.80 per cent GS 2021	7.8	11 April 2011	11 April 2021	67,492.66
7.94 per cent GS 2021	7.94	24 May 2006	24 May 2021	49,425
10.25 per cent GS 2021	10.25	30 May 2001	30 May 2021	26,213.32
8.79 per cent GS 2021	8.79	8 November 2011	8 November 2021	83,000
8.20 per cent GS 2022	8.2	15 February 2007	15 February 2022	57,632.33
8.35 per cent GS 2022	8.35	14 May 2002	14 May 2022	77,000
8.15 per cent GS 2022	8.15	11 June 2012	11 June 2022	83,000
8.08 per cent GS 2022	8.08	02 August 2007	02 August 2022	68,969.41
5.87 per cent GS 2022 (conv)	5.87	28 August 2003	28 August 2022	11,000
8.13 per cent GS 2022	8.13	21 September 2007	21 September 2022	70,495.28
6.84 per cent GS 2022	6.84	12 September 2016	19 December 2022	99,000
6.30 per cent GS 2023	6.30	9 April 2003	09 April 2023	13,000

Nomenclature	*Coupon (%)*	*Date of First Issue*	*Date of Maturity*	*Outstanding Stock (in ₹, in crore)*
7.37 per cent GS 2023	7.37	16 April 2018	16 April 2023	39,987.81
7.16 per cent GS 2023	7.16	20 May 2013	20 May 2023	77,100
1.44 per cent II GS 2023	1.44	5 June 2013	5 June 2023	1,235.14
6.17 per cent GS 2023 (conv)	6.17	12 June 2003	12 June 2023	14,000
8.83 per cent GS 2023	8.83	25 November 2013	25 November 2023	83,000
7.68 per cent GS 2023	7.68	27 April 2015	15 December 2023	88,132.01
Inflation Indexed National Savings Securities-Cumulative (IINSS-C) 1.5 per cent GS 2023	1.50	25 December 2013	25 December 2023	71.08
7.32 per cent GS 2024	7.32	28 January 2019	28 January 2024	4,000.00
7.35 per cent GS 2024	7.35	22 June 2009	22 June 2024	90,168.02
8.40 per cent GS 2024	8.40	28 July 2014	28 July 2024	90,000.00
FRB 2024	6.38	7 November 2016	7 November 2024	1,16,965.03
9.15 per cent GS 2024	9.15	14 November 2011	14 November 2024	92,000.00

Source: Based on author's analysis of data from Department of Economic Affairs, Government of India

The cost of the borrowing programme also becomes critical given the economic disruption caused by COVID-19. Figure 7.6 shows debt as a percentage of the GDP for several emerging market economies. There is a jump in 2020 for most economies as the level of economic activity contracted while, on the other hand, governments borrowed extensively to provide some form of stimulus to their respective economies. For most countries, IMF projects the debt levels to moderate except for China, Brazil, South Africa and Turkey. Figure 7.6 also provides us with a comparative assessment of India with respect to some of its comparable economies. India is not one of the economies with relatively high debt or low debt to GDP, as the value continues to hover between 50–80 per cent.

FIGURE 7.6: *Debt as a Percentage of GDP for Various Countries*

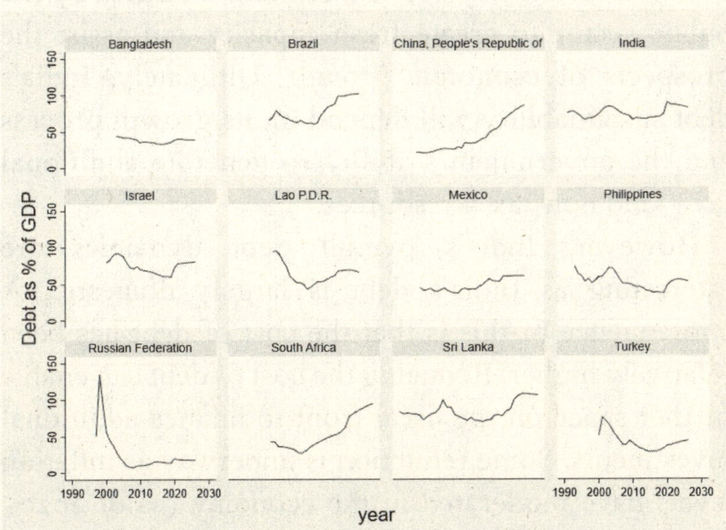

Source: Based on author's analysis of data from *International Financial Statistics*, IMF

Concluding Observations

Public debt is often viewed as undesirable and governments try to reduce it over time. Despite this, most countries do have extensive borrowing programmes as they are necessitated by the need to make critical investments and provision for several public goods. Thus, public debt is used to create public good. However, public debt by itself is a source of a public good, given that it serves as an important source of risk-free assets in the economy. It is therefore important to not restrict the understanding of public debt as just a means to finance excess government spending. This is critical for economies such as India, which are still developing and require massive investments in physical, natural and human capital. These investments have to be financed largely by the public sector to create fresh capacity and assist the prospects of economic growth. Ultimately, India's debt sustainability will depend on its growth process and the government's ability to generate additional tax—and non-tax—resources.

However, India's overall debt dynamics are interesting as India's debt is largely domestic. A consequence of this is that the cost of debt has been relatively higher. Reducing the cost of debt can enable further space on the fiscal front to finance additional investments. Some reduction is underway as inflation levels have moderated in the economy (as of 2020–2021) and subsequently, interest rates too have moderated, bringing down the cost of fresh borrowings. However, there is a need to accelerate the process of replacing high-cost sovereign borrowings with low-cost short-term borrowings.

Overall, the level of India's public debt has remained stable despite COVID-19 and the country is expected to register strong growth in the foreseeable future. Strong growth should absorb any pandemic-induced impact on the general build-up of sovereign debt in the system.

Kautilya's Views

It is in this broad context of debt dynamics and sustainability that one needs to look at Kautilya's views on the subject. While there is much discussion on personal debt and the recovery of debt, the emphasis on sovereign debt needs to be explored further. This could be challenging given that the idea of a sovereign state in Kautilyan times is quite different to what we have today. Therefore, the concepts and implications of sovereign debt might also be quite different. We look at some basic questions that could be explored further to extract Kautilya's views on this.

Questions for Kautilya

1. From the nation's point of view (not the individual), what would be Kautilya's view on debt sustainability? Is debt an inherent taboo or

does he see it as a vehicle for future growth, like how modern economies function?

2. What is his view on the idea of debt sustainability? How would he define it? What are the parameters that he would consider?
3. What about an unforeseen event such as the pandemic? Will Kautilya follow the model that he has for natural calamities (which is the state intervening and supporting the people) or would he tweak his thinking to suit something as customised as a pandemic?
4. Does he have any view on the composition of debt that the sovereign can take to finance such events?
5. What would be his proposals for paying off this debt in the long run?

8

Summary and Insights

Kautilyanomics has many dimensions and perspectives that need to be explored. Through this book, I have attempted to define Kautilya's worldview with a semblance of a structure that is relatable to our times. As I mentioned at the beginning of the book, this is a challenging task on many fronts. First, the *Arthashastra* text by its nature is a long-form poetical treatise that is not aligned to modern-day structures, with a dense linguistic text that can be interpreted in numerous ways by different scholars. Second, the context of the text is very different compared to that of today. Obviously, we live in a very different world powered by technology, which wasn't there in ancient times. However, despite these challenges, I have tried to create a structure. Now, I will try to provide a chapter-by-chapter summary followed by answers to some fundamental questions that we can decipher from these chapters.

THE CONCEPTUAL UNDERPINNING OF KAUTILYA'S ECONOMIC WORLDVIEW

In the conceptual framework chapter, we discussed the idea of dharmic capitalism as the central structure of Kautilya's thinking. In comparing this with conventional frameworks such as Keynesian and laissez-faire approaches, we showcased the way dharmic capitalism functions. Kautilya envisaged the idea of dharmic capitalism based on the foundation of dharma and characterised by the prism of ethics, responsibilities and social harmony.

As seen in the chapter, the three pillars of dharmic capitalism are a rule-based yet non-intrusive state, wealth creation through a global look and sustainable growth and welfare. Unlike the mainstream frameworks, the role of dharma becomes central to the functioning of dharmic capitalism. If the foundations of dharma are solid, according to Kautilya, the seamlessness of dharmic capitalism endures regardless of the state/non-state interventions (or lack thereof) based approaches of mainstream frameworks. The state and the market would co-exist on the foundation of dharma.

Wealth Creation as a Part of the Kautilyan Framework

In this section on wealth creation, we looked at the role of international and domestic trade, gold accumulation in India and savings as an instrument of growth in the country. These are themes that are unique to India and hence chosen as part of the chapters in the book.

In all of these, we noticed that Kautilya was very open to trading with the international partners yet wanted to keep checks and balances in place. His ideas of reduction in trade barriers, promotion of internal trade within the kingdom and the need to calibrate tariff management to facilitate trade all echo some of the ideas that are being applied today.

Consumer savings and investment also play an important role in India's economic activity. Given the high savings rates coupled with informality and community-based savings and credits systems, this dynamic is unique in India compared to other countries of similar size. We also discussed how Kautilya would have recommended utilising household savings potential to boost investment. Here, we looked at the idea of gold as an investment rather than a consumption good.

The idea of transitioning from unsecured debt (created by informal savings channels) to more secure debt was also an idea that Kautilya might have recommended. Since he reiterated the need for financial stability, he would have preferred a more secure debt. We had also discussed the idea of tax breaks to boost investment—something that Kautilya would have done given that he had himself employed sector and activity-based tax breaks for some business segments as shown earlier. Lastly, the role of innovation in boosting investment was also another Kautilyan feature that might resonate today.

We also discussed the idea of gold, which is unique to India's current economic structure. It would have been fascinating to see how Kautilya would have advised in such a scenario—would he advocate for more gold accumulation or would he look at other sources of investment? Either way, my sense is that he would have chosen the more pragmatic of the two. The massive consumption of gold in India with an inversely proportional domestic production has left a supply-demand gap that needs to be filled. We also explored the Kautilyan ideas of the consumer being king, greater supply-chain coordination and the ability to leverage market power for the benefit of the country.

Sustainable Growth and Welfare in the Kautilyan Framework

In the section on sustainable growth and welfare, we segregated the discussion into two main components—sustainable growth and welfare. Kautilya's approach towards sustainable growth was directly contrasted with what is currently happening in India. Developments in sanitation, toilet construction and the thrust on renewable energy were highlighted in this section. In contrast, we also looked at Kautilya's approach, which had three key pillars—societal, environmental and familial responsibilities. The societal responsibilities pillar focused on Kautilya's views on biodiversity and a common civic sense/mission to have sustainable growth. On environmental responsibilities, we also looked at the emphasis given by Kautilya on the protection and development of forests, animal welfare and water management respectively. And we looked at similar contemporary approaches.

On welfare, we looked at community-based financing, which was unique to India, and also the current inequality trends based on some of the literature and my recent work on the subject. This addresses the broader issue of inequality and provides a Kautilyan view of it. We elaborated on the concept of matsya nyaya here and highlighted the need to protect the vulnerable from the 'big fish'. Kautilya's thinking on minimum wage, targeted welfare and incentive-based appraisals were pointed out to show how he would have addressed these issues if he had been a policymaker today. Moreover, there was a parallel drawn to some of the recent schemes, including the direct benefit transfer (DBT) scheme which has been successful in the transfer of income to the poor in recent years.

How a Rule-based Yet Non-intrusive State Fits into Kautilya's Thinking

This is a question that is addressed across the book in various chapters, albeit specifically in the chapter on rule of law and enforcement of contracts. In this section, we further elaborate on the concept of matsya nyaya and introduce the idea of dandaneeti to maintain yogakshema. The former is the principle and the latter is the vehicle with the bigger goal of yogakshema at play.

We looked at the Kautilyan philosophy of kinship (its affiliation to the state) and principles of property and labour laws and contracts. These included details on common, collective and private property laws, contractual and collective labour contracts, and their respective enforcement strategies. By distinguishing between the nuances of the legislation and the implementation, we also provided some perspective on the role of enforcement of contracts in ensuring a thriving economy.

Criss-crossing into today's times, a detailed case study on the IBC process was discussed and Kautilya's thinking was adapted to the solutions to make the process better. Through this process, we also looked at the role of debt repayment methods and strategies adopted by Kautilya in the Mauryan kingdom. This would also include the SDBD approach to debt resolution, which is often used indirectly in corporate restructurings. Furthermore, we also learned about Kautilya's idea of sequencing debt resolution into different parts to ensure that there is an incentive for the debtor to pay back the debt in a gradual manner. In retrospect, these techniques provided a fresh perspective on how Kautilya would have handled the enforcement of contracts. Most importantly, it highlighted the common thread of a state which is strong on its rules and its implementation but non-intrusive in the day-to-day functioning of government activities.

A summary of these insights is highlighted succinctly in Table 8.1.

TABLE 8.1: *A Summary of Insights from the Book*

Themes	*Chapters*	*Current Ideas and Perspectives*	*Kautilyan-era Ideas and Perspectives*	*Kautilya Tantra*
Overview	Introduction	Pre-Kautilyan Era		
Overview and translations	The *Arthashastra*—Questions, Answers and Translations	Q and A	Tantrayukti and the challenge of translation	
Philosophy of dharmic capitalism	Philosophical Frameworks	Keynesian and laissez-faire	Dharmic capitalism	Dharmic capitalism through a rule-based yet non-intrusive state, wealth creation and sustainable growth and welfare
Wealth creation	Trade	Current perspective on international trade along with historical trade measures compiled by Angus Maddison	Ancient trade networks, corporate guilds and maritime routes in the Kautilyan era	Ease of trade, internal trade between states/kingdom and export diversification along with tariff management
	Gold	Historical perspective, gold supply and demand composition and the GDS scheme in India	Perspective on historical gold accumulation	Key themes such as consumer is king, coordinated supply chains and the need to leverage market power

Themes	*Chapters*	*Current Ideas and Perspectives*	*Kautilyan-era Ideas and Perspectives*	*Kautilya Tantra*
	Savings, Investment and Growth (SIG)	Literature on SIG, the trends and composition of SIG in India, the role of household savings and the GFCF trends.		Key themes such as savings as a driver of investment, the transition from unsecured to secure debt, the role of tax breaks for investment and innovation to drive SIG
Sustainable growth and welfare	Sustainable Growth	Recent developments including the Swachh Bharat initiative, sanitation drive, construction of toilets and the Jal Jeevan Mission	Societal responsibilities including biodiversity and civic sense/mission towards sustainable growth. Environmental responsibilities including forest maintenance, animal welfare and water management	A holistic approach towards sustainable development, which encompasses societal, environmental and familial responsibilities
	Welfare/ Redistribution	Recent trends on inequality and redistributive dynamics in India	Concept of matsya nyaya discussed	Key ideas such as flexible minimum wage, targeting welfare mechanisms and outcome-based incentives for wealth transfer

Themes	*Chapters*	*Current Ideas and Perspectives*	*Kautilyan-era Ideas and Perspectives*	*Kautilya Tantra*
Rule-based Yet Non-intrusive State	Rule of Law and Enforcement of Contracts	The IBC	Concepts of kingship, property, labour laws were discussed along with enforcement actions. Moreover, debt recovery principles were also discussed.	Debt recovery through techniques such as SDBD and sequencing of debt resolution in a phased manner

POST-PANDEMIC WORLD AND KAUTILYA'S THINKING

We had briefly touched upon topics that could be of interest in the years ahead in a post-pandemic world. These topics were changing demographic trends with an ageing population, the emergence of AI and its consequence for the working-age population and the role of debt sustainability in the decade ahead. These are interesting ideas that could play an important role for India in the coming decades. While I am still seeking solutions through the Kautilyan lens for these, one wonders how Kautilya would have approached them if he were a policymaker today.

Kautalyan Relevance

In retrospect, one needs to get back to the questions that I posed in the introductory part of the book to assess the relevance of Kautilya in today's times. Those questions are the following:

1. What is the relevance of Kautilya's broad thematic principles/frameworks in today's times?
2. What is the relevance of the concepts used during Kautilya's times and their impact now?
3. How relevant is Kautilya's thinking to some of the contemporary challenges that we see today?

As seen in each of the pillars of dharmic capitalism, the broad thematic philosophical frameworks are different, but not irrelevant, to current frameworks.

While the Western orientation is largely based on the role of the state versus the market (Keynesian and laissez-faire), dharmic capitalism incorporates the idea of dharma at its core. Dharma is the foundation on which the role of the state, markets and other factors are built. Given the structural challenges in the binary state versus market markets approaches, especially post the global financial crisis and its after-effects, there is a growing thrust for an alternative system that could encompass a variety of challenges beyond the narrow state versus market paradigm.

In terms of concepts, many of the economic principles that we have today were used in Kautilyan times and some of them are as significant today. These include ease of doing business and trade, consumer protection, coordinated supply chains, tax breaks, leveraging market power, flexible minimum wage, sustainable development strategies and debt resolution, among others. While most of these concepts are no doubt more refined in modern times, one can't help but be amazed by how these were used thousands of years ago.

The lack of sophisticated data systems (or at least our perception of them) makes it even more intriguing how some of these concepts were applied at a practical level for policymaking. Kautilya's approach to these concepts certainly makes one think about its possible impact in today's times. While the complexity and breadth of the applications of these concepts might vary, the thinking behind them doesn't seem to be far off from contemporary theories. There is also a strong sense that these concepts were well thought out in the ancient world.

Finally, in terms of Kautilya's thinking—the frameworks, the conceptual underpinnings and the entire gamut defined as Kautilyanomics—and its relevance to addressing present-day challenges, Table 8.1 is more than illustrative of its relevance to present-day challenges. If we simplify this further and look at a few macro challenges that confront the world, it is even more striking. Let's take the challenges of sustainable growth, inequality, climate change and corruption to name a few. If one thinks about a common thread that connects the solution to these challenges, the answer invariably goes back to society. For us to deal with sustainable growth, people must prioritize the 'big picture' and think about the impact it has on other citizens in their countries as well as the planet. The same goes for climate change since without prioritizing or caring about the 'society-at-large and the planet', one can't find sustainable solutions. Even for inequality, without having the mentality of taking care of their own kith-and-kin and the rest of the community, i.e., societal responsibilities, there wouldn't be a social buy-in to address redistribution concerns. And how are we going to address all this without a corruption-free society? The role of ethics in society plays an important role in addressing this. While the market and the state can be facilitators of policy change, unless the society is built to nurture its responsibilities to promote harmony for the people and the planet as a whole, in an ethical manner along with the state and the markets, it would be difficult to address some of the challenges mentioned earlier. In simpler terms, dharmic capitalism as a concept is more relevant today than it has ever been.

Not only does dharmic capitalism attempt to address some of these challenges, but it also rests on a firm foundation of dharma that the other approaches lack. To this extent, in my view, Kautilyanomics, powered by dharmic capitalism, offers a fresh perspective that is not just relevant but is a viable alternative system for the modern age.

In retrospect, a few things stand out about Kautilyanomics for me. First, not only was Kautilya ahead of his time in his understanding of economics than historical thinkers such as Adam Smith, but he was also a practical policy economist who kept the people's welfare on top of his mind. Second, his concepts and ideas were similar to some of the concepts that are being used today albeit with different levels of complexity given the differences in the context. Lastly, Kautilyanomics as a whole has many lessons and possible solutions for the modern age in addressing some of its contemporary challenges. Most of all, it does provide a much-needed fresh perspective on addressing some of the challenges that India may face in the years ahead.

THE ROAD AHEAD

As I mentioned in the introductory chapter, this has been a journey of exploration to understand the *Arthashastra* and its economic relevance. This book is a small part of the bigger journey. One of my main objectives was to decipher a coherent framework for Kautilya's economic policies and I believe this book takes a step in that direction. However, there are many more things to explore, and I hope to provide further details in the future about Kautilya's thinking on a variety of socio-economic issues. Besides working further on the translations, I hope to analyse more futuristic issues through the lens of these ideas in the coming years. There is also the ambition to study the broader puranic literature to interpret the economic geniuses of those times, especially in the common era age. It remains to be seen what shape it would take and what areas it would cover but I am very interested in pursuing an intellectual sequel to this book which covers a broader and a more contemporaneous economic canvas through a historical lens.

If you have read the book up to this page, I sincerely hope that I have enhanced your curiosity about Kautilya and made you think about the issues that were discussed in the book. Some well-wishers who have read this book wanted me to write it with a bit more forceful tone instead of staying largely tone-neutral throughout the book except for the last few pages. However, it was a conscious attempt on my part. I firmly believe that the facts will speak for themselves especially when they are not thrust upon.

The need for debate and discussion on Kautilya's ideas arises out of exposure to these facts which will lead to the production of more literature on the subject. He might be wrong on some occasions and right on others, but he was a visionary whose ideas were much ahead of his time and remain relevant even today. I hope you gained an insight into the sheer breadth of his thinking. The purpose was to take you on a journey to discover Kautilya's relevance for today's socio-economic issues and provide a perspective on the visionary that he was.

I hope Kautilyanomics served this purpose!

Copyright Acknowledgements

Grateful acknowledgement is made to the following for permission to reprint copyright material:

Balbir S. Sihag for tables from his book Kautilya: The True Founder of Economics published in 2014 by Vitasta

L.N. Rangarajan for tables from his book Kautilya: The Arthashastra published in 1992 by Penguin Random House India

Sumedha Verma Ojha for a map from 'Uttarapath and Dakshinapath: The Great Trade Routes of Jambudwipa' published on 12 August 2016 by Swarajya

Professor Satish Deodhar, Dr Sushrutha S. and Karan Bhasin for co-authoring a section each with the author

While all efforts have been made to trace copyright holders and obtain permission, this has not been possible in all cases; any omissions brought to our attention will be remedied in future editions.

ACKNOWLEDGEMENTS

There are many people who I need to thank. First and foremost, my family (my wife and my parents) for their support. My wife, Lakshmi, for her patience in dealing with me by spending many hours on the book and providing invaluable inputs whenever needed. My gratitude to my parents, Sharadha Balasubramanian and R. Balasubramanian, without whose upbringing and value systems I wouldn't be in a position to write this much on any subject. Many others have played an important part in this exercise.

I would like to thank Bloomsbury publishers for providing me with the opportunity to pursue this project. Kudos to Praveen Tiwari at Bloomsbury for being a pillar of support and a staunch motivator for this book. I have asked him numerous questions in the process of working on it, and he has always been patient in responding to them with a calm and confident demeanour, no matter how silly the questions were. Besides Praveen, other staff members of Bloomsbury—Shreya Chakrabarti, Nitin Valecha and Gauri Kelkar—were also very helpful through the drafting–publication cycle.

I also must thank Prakash Loungani, Cyrus Rustomjee and Michael Kell for supporting me and giving me the freedom to pursue this personal project.

Professor Balbir Singh Sihag and Professor Satish Deodhar have been instrumental in providing me with the intellectual and analytical motivation to pursue this project. I would like to also thank the various translators of the *Arthashastra* text; without their work, my task would have been much more challenging. I re-learnt (and I am still learning) Samskritam through the spoken classes of Raghuvarma Basavaraj (based out of Jericho Island in New Jersey, USA) under the aegis of Samskrita Bharati. He teaches Samskritam to hundreds of students (young and old) free of charge with a dedicative zeal that is unparalleled. Without this knowledge, it would have been much harder to analyse the text, so 'dhanyavadaha' to his yeoman service!

Hari Kiran Vadlamani from Indic Academy has been a constant pillar of support for the book, and I am grateful for his drive and motivation. H.K.V. Garu is another selfless warrior who has helped many authors over the years. I would like to thank Dr Bibek Debroy for being kind enough to write the foreword of the book. I have always admired his writings on ancient history and his economic ideas over the years. He was one of the first people to read the manuscript and provide valuable comments. In this context, I want to also thank J.R. Rao, a family friend and mentor, from the International Finance Corporation. He read the manuscript in just a couple of days and provided some insightful comments. His guidance and support are always appreciable. I am also grateful to those who were kind enough to provide comments and blurbs for the book, including Niranjan Rajadhyaksha, Lord

Meghnad Desai, Shekhar Gupta, Surjit Bhalla, Indermit Gill and Sanjeev Sanyal among others. I am grateful to them for giving some of their precious time to the manuscript and providing valuable comments. I must also mention and appreciate Sanjeev Sanyal's support for my work since my first book. His humility and ability to research economic history have always been an inspiration. Others who I must thank include Dr Sushrutha S. from Amritha Vishwa Vidyapeetham (he was formerly with MIT School of Vedic Sciences) for providing guidance on Samskritam and translation challenges of the text, Karan Bhasin for co-authoring the section on debt sustainability and providing inputs on some of the other chapters, Professor Krishnamurthy Ramasubramanian (professor at IIT Bombay) for his guidance and instilling the importance of learning Samskritam properly while working on the text, Viswanathan S. (publisher of business magazine *Industrial Economist*) who gave me the first opportunity to write on a public platform many years ago. My gratitude is due also to all those unsung well-wishers who have helped me in the process of writing this book but have not found their names mentioned here.

Lastly, I would like to thank my late grandmother, Jambakam Ramamurthy, for making me who I am today. I have dedicated this book to her because without her upbringing, grace and support, I would not be where I am today. She was aware of the book and would constantly motivate me to complete it even though she was in her 90s. Her relentless zeal for socio-political issues along with her ability to write, read and motivate people were inspirational. I will be eternally grateful to her for many lifetimes to come. I know that wherever she is, she will be beaming with pride and joy upon seeing the completion of this book.

BIBLIOGRAPHY

Abhyanker, V. and K.V. Abhyanker. 1916. *Mudraraksasam: A Complete Text* (original playwright Visakhadatta). Ahmedabad: Nandlal C. Bodiwala.

Ahluwalia, M.S. 2002. 'Economic Reforms in India Since 1991: Has Gradualism Worked?' *Journal of Economic Perspectives*, 16 (3): 67–88. Available at https://www.aeaweb.org/articles?id=10.1257/089533002760278721

Ahluwalia, M.S. 2001. 'State-Level Performance under Economic Reforms in India.' Stanford King Center on Global Development Working Paper, Institute for Economic Policy Research, Stanford, USA. Available at https://siepr.stanford.edu/research/publications/state-level-performance-under-economic-reforms-india

Ahluwalia, M.S. 2019. 'India's Economic Reforms Achievements and Next Steps'. Available at https://onlinelibrary.wiley.com/doi/abs/10.1111/aepr.12239

Aiyar, Swaminathan. 2016. 'Twenty-Five Years of Indian Economic Reform'. Policy Analysis No. 803, Cato Institute. Available at https://www.cato.org/policy-analysis/twenty-five-years-indian-economic-reform.

Ambedkar, B.R. 1946. 'Shudras and Dasas', Part I, Chapter VI, Section IV. In *Who Were the Shudras?* Available at http//www.ambedkar.org/ambcd/38B2.%20Who %20were%20the%20 Shudras%20 PART%20I.htm (accessed on 9 May 2020).

Anwar, Shakeel. 2017. 'Maurya Empire: A Detailed Summary'. Jagran Josh. Available at https//www.jagranjosh.com/general-knowledge/maurya-empire-a-detailed-summary-1467280009-1

Badarinza, C., V. Balasubramanian, V. and T. Ramadorai. 2019. 'The Household Finance Landscape in Emerging Economies', WBS Finance Group Research Paper Series, No. 257.

Balaji, K. and R. Maheswari. 2014. 'A Paradigm Shift in Buying Behavior of Indians Towards Gold Jewellery—A Theoretical

Approach with Reference to Growth of Branded Retailers', *Indian Journal of Applied Research*, February, 4 (2).

Balasubramanian, Sriram, R. Kumar and P. Loungani. 2021. Inequality and Locational Determinants of the Distribution of Living Standards in India. International Monetary Fund (IMF) Working Paper 21/50.

Balasubramanian, Sriram and Paul Anthony Cashin. 2019. 'Gross National Happiness and Macroeconomic Indicators in the Kingdom of Bhutan', IMF Working Paper, No. 19/15, International Monetary Fund, USA, January.

Bandhyopadhyaya, Narayan Chandra. 1927. *Kautilya or an Exposition of His Social Ideal and Political Theory*. Calcutta: R. Cambray and Company.

Barro, R.J. 1990. 'Government Spending in a Simple Model of Endogenous Growth'. *Journal of Political Economy*, 98 (55): 103–125.

Basham, A.L. 1959. *The Wonder That Was India*. New York: Grove Press.

Bhalla, S.S. 2003. *Imagine There's No Country Poverty, Inequality and Growth in the Era of Globalisation*. New Delhi: Penguin Books.

Bhandarkar, D.R. 1990 (reprint). *Lectures on Ancient Indian Numismatics: The Carmichael Lectures, 1921*.

Bathla, Kumar. 2019. 'For Indian Farmers, Direct Benefit Transfers Can Work Better Than Fertilizer Subsidies'. International Food Policy Research Institute.

Bhattacharya, S. 2014. 'Forest and Biodiversity Conservation in Ancient Indian Culture: A Review Based on Old Texts and Archaeological Evidences'. *International Letters of Social and Humanistic Sciences*, 30: 35–46.

Billington, R. 1997. *Understanding Eastern Philosophy*. London: Routledge.

Boesche, R. 2003. *The First Great Political Realist Kautilya and His Arthashastra*. Lanham: MD Lexington Books.

Boulding, K. 1981. *A Preface to Grants Economics: The Economy of Love and Fear*. New York: Praeger.

Bowie, N. and R. Simon. 1977. *The Individual and the Political Order*. New York: Prentice-Hall.

Brockington, J. 1998. *The Sanskrit Epics*. Boston: Brill Academic.

Broom, D. 2020. '6 of the World's 10 Most Polluted Cities Are in India'. World Economic Forum, 5 March. Available at https://www.weforum.org/agenda/2020/03/6-of-the-world-s-10-most-polluted-cities-are-in-india/

Chickermane, Gautam. 2020. 'An Intellectual Biography of India's New Agri Reforms'. News18, 14 December. Available at: https//www.news18.com/news/opinion/an-intellectual-biography-of-indias-new-agri-reforms-3173069.html

Chitrav, S. 1998. *Rigvedache Marathi Bhashantar* (*Rigveda in Marathi*). Pune: Bharatiya Charitrakosh Mandal.

Churiwal, A. and A. Shreni. 2012. 'Cognizant 20-20 Insights: Surveying the Indian Gold Loan Market'. Cognizant Business Consulting.

Dasgupta, A. 1993. *A History of Indian Economic Thought*. London: Routledge.

Datta, B. 1927. 'Discussions on the Origin and Development of the Idea of "Percent"'. *American Mathematical Monthly*, 34 (10): 530–531.

Debroy, Bibek. forthcoming (2022). *Vishnu Purana* (translation). New Delhi: Penguin Random House.

Deodhar, S. 2019. *Economic Sutra Ancient Indian Antecedents to Economic Thought*. Gurugram: Penguin Random House.

Deodhar, S. and S. Balasubramanian. 2020. 'The Pre-Kautilyan Period: A Sustainable Model through Ancient Economic Ideas and Practices'. European Historical Economics Society (EHES) Working Paper, No. 199, EHES, Austria.

Kohli, Atul. 2006, 'Politics of Economic Growth in India, 1980-2005: Part I: The 1980s', *Economic and Political Weekly*, 1251–1259.

Frank, R. 2001. Luxury Fever: Why Money Fails to Satisfy in an Era of Excess. New York: Free Press.

Fukuyama, F. 1996. *Trust: The Social Virtues and the Creation of Prosperity*. New York: Simon and Shuster.

Ganguli, K.M. *Mahabharata: Shanti Parva (Book 12)*, Sections 8, 76, 88 and 188. Available on 1896a. http//www.sacred-texts.com/hin/m12/m12b015.htm

Ganguli, K.M. 2005. *The Complete Mahabharata in 4 Volumes Translated into English Prose from the Original Sanskrit Text.*

Ghisellini, F. and Chang, B. 2018. *Behavioral Economics Moving Forward*. Cham, Switzerland: Palgrave Macmillan.

Ghosh Ray, R. 1996. 'The Attitude of Kautilya to Aranya'. *Environment and History* 2, June (2): 221–229.

Gokhale, M. 2018. 'The Economic Condition of India in the Days of Epic'. In *Socio-Economic Dynamics of Indian Culture: A Historical Overview*, edited by A. Tilak, D. Jawane, N. Chitnis and R. Vaishampayan, 103. Mumbai: Hindusthan Prakashan Sanstha.

Gopalakrishnan, P., S. Mathur, P. Rath, A. Vats and T. Ramodorai. 2017. 'Household Finance Committee Report'. Government of India.

Government of India. 2015–16. 'Spreading JAM across India's Economy'. Economic Survey, Government of India, 50.

Government of India. Swachch Bharat Mission. Available at https//swachhbharatmission.gov.in/SBMCMS/about-us.htm

Goyal, M. 2020. 'Borrowed Joy: Decoding the Digital Credit Boom of India'. *The Economic Times*, 3 March.

Griffith, R. 1895. *Hymns of the Atharvaveda*. Sacred Text Archive. Available at http//www.sacred-texts.com/hin/av/av03004.htm

Griffith, R. 1886. *The Rig Veda*. Sacred Text Archive. Available at http//www. sacred-texts.com/hin/rigveda/ (accessed on 4 May).

Griffith, R. 1899. *The Texts of the White Yajurveda*. Sacred Text Archive. Available at https//www.sacred-texts.com/hin/wyv/index.htm

Haque, Y.A. 2019. 'Swachh Bharat Success Goes beyond Just Toilets and India'. *Forbes* India, 19 September.

Hebalkar, S. 2018. 'Trade Routes of Ancient India'. Available at http//indiaconnectingworld.com/trade-routes-of-ancient-india/

Helliwell, J., R. Layard, and J. Sachs. 2016. World Happiness Report 2016, Update, Vol. I. New York Sustainable Development Solutions Network.

IITK. 2020. *Valmiki Ramayana*. Developed and Maintained by the Indian Institute of Technology Kanpur (IITK). Available at https//www.valmiki.iitk.ac.in/ (accessed on 2 May 2020) and https//valmikiramayan.net/index.html

Indo-Asian News Service (IANS). 2019. 'Over ₹1 Lakh Crore Deposited in Pradhan Mantri Jan Dhan Yojana Accounts, Reveals RTI'. *India Today*. Available at https://www.indiatoday.in/india/story/over-rs-1-lakh-crore-deposited-in-pradhan-mantri-jan-dhan-yojana-accounts-reveals-rti-1581820-2019-08-17

Insolvency and Bankruptcy Board of India. About Us. Available at https//www.ibbi.gov.in/about.

International Monetary Fund. 2021. 'Policy Responses to COVID-19', July. Available at https//www.imf.org/en/Topics/imf-and-covid19/Policy-Responses-to-COVID-19#I

Jain, L. 1929. *Indigenous Banking in India*. London: Macmillan and Co.

Kane, P.V. 1941. *History of Dharmashastra*, Vol 2, Part 1. Pune: Bhandarkar Oriental Research Institute.

Kangle, R. 1965. *Kautilya Arthashastra*, Part 3. New Delhi: Motilal Banarsidass Publishers.

Kangle, R. 1965. *The Kautilya Arthasastra*, Edition 1, Part 1 (Sanskrit), Part 2 (Translation) and Part 3 (Commentary). New Delhi: Motilal Banarsidass Publishers.

Kautilya. Matsya Nyaya. Available at: https://dharmakshethra.com/matsya-nyaya/

Kazanas, Nicholas. 2010. 'Ṛgveda 7.95.2 and Karen Thomson'. *The Journal of Indo-European Studies*, 38 (3–4): 409–421.

Keynes, J.M. 1973 (1936). *The General Theory of Employment, Interest, and Money*, 7. Available at: https://www.files.ethz.ch/isn/125515/1366_KeynesTheoryofEmployment.pdf

Knapp, S. 2006. *The Power of the Dharma: An Introduction to Hinduism and Vedic Culture*. New York: iUniverse.

Kochhar, Kalpana, Utsav Kumar, Raghuram Rajan, Arvind Subramanian et all. 2006. 'India's Pattern of Development: What Happened, What Follows?'. *Journal of Monetary Economics*, 53(5): 981–1,019.

Kohli, A. 2006. 'Politics of Economic Growth in India, 1980–2005. Part I: The 1980s'. Available at: https://www.princeton.edu/~kohli/docs/PEGI_PartI.pdf

Kohli, A. 2006. 'Politics of Economic Growth in India, 1980–2005. Part II: The 1990s and Beyond'. Available at https://www.princeton.edu/~kohli/docs/PEGI_PartII.pdf

Kulke, H. and D. Rothermund. 2016. *A History of India*, Edition 4. London: Routledge.

Kundu, A. 2019. 'Are Indians Moving More Freely within the Country'. *The Hindustan Times*, New Delhi, 3 January.

Kone, Zovanga L., Maggie Y. Liu, Aaditya Mattoo, Çağlar Ozden, et al. 2017. 'Internal Borders and Migration in India'. Policy Research Working Paper, Development Research Group, World Bank Group. Available at http//documents.worldbank.org/curated/en/389841511186819498/pdf/WPS8244.pdf).

Lucas, R. 1988. 'On the Mechanics of Economic Development'. *Journal of Monetary Economics*, 22: 3–42.

MacDonnell, A. and A. Keith. 1912. *Vedic Index of Names and Subjects*. London: John Murray.

Madan, G. 1981. *Economic Thinking in India*. New Delhi: S. Chand and Co.

Maddison, A. 2001. *The World Economy: A Millennial Perspective*. London: Oxford Publishers.

Mahadevan, T. 1960. *Outlines of Hinduism*. Bombay: Chetana Ltd.

Mahulikar, G. 2018. 'Economic Thought in Kautilya's *Arthashastra*'. In *Socio-Economic Dynamics of Indian Culture: A Historical Overview*, edited by A. Tilak, D. Jawane, N. Chitnis and R. Vaishampayan. Mumbai: Hindusthan Prakashan Sanstha.

Majumdar, R. 1918. *Corporate Life in Ancient India*. London: Forgotten Books.

Majumdar, R. 1922. *Corporate Life in Ancient India*, Second Edition. Calcutta: Calcutta University. Available at https//archive.org/details/corporatelifeinaoomajurich/page/n9

McKechnie, W. 1896. *The State and the Individual*. Glasgow: James McLehose and Sons.

Mehta, T. 1999. *Sanskrit Play Production in Ancient India*. Delhi: Motilal Banarsidass.

Mishra, P., J. Das and S. Mishra. 2010. 'The Dynamics of Savings and Investment Relationship in India.' *European Journal of Economics, Finance and Administrative Science*, February, 18: 163–72.

Moore, K. and S. Reid. 2008. 'The Birth of Brand: 4000 Years of Branding History'. Paper No. 10169, Munich Personal RePEc Archive (MPRA), Germany. Available at https://mpra.ub.uni-muenchen.de/10169/ (accessed on 9 May 2020).

Mukerji, S. 1963. 'The Republican Trends in Ancient India'. PhD thesis, Hari Singh Gour University, Sagar, Madhya Pradesh.

Müller, M. 1879. *Katha-Upanishad*, Adhyaya I, Valli I, Verses 1–4. Sacred Text Archive. Available at http//www.sacred-texts.com/hin/sbe15/sbe15010.htm (accessed on 5 May 2020).

Nadkarni, M. 2012. 'Hindu Economic Philosophy'. In *Oxford Handbook of Hindu Economics and Business*, edited by H. Vinod. New Delhi: Oxford University Press.

Nair, Vishwanath. 2021. 'Four Years On, Did RBI's IBC Gamble with 40 Large Defaulters Work?'. Bloomberg Quint, 14 June. Available at https://www.bloombergquint.com/business/four-years-on-did-rbis-ibc-gamble-with-40-large-defaulters-work

Narayanan, P., G. Balagopal and A. Sahay. 2015. 'Understanding the Government's Attempt to Transform Attitudes Towards a Critical Resource: Gold Monetization in India'. Available at. https://ideas.repec.org/a/eee/jrpoli/v66y2020ics0301420719305501.html

Narayanan, K. 2013. Press Information Bureau, Government of India. Available at: https//pib.gov.in/newsite/mbErel.aspx?relid=92113

Nehru, Jawaharlal. 1946. *Discovery of India*. Calcutta: Signet Press. Available at: https// archive.org/details/DiscoveryOfIndia (accessed on 9 May 2020).

NITI Aayog. 2018. 'National Strategy for Artificial Intelligence'. NITI Aayog Discussion Paper Series, NITI Aayog, New Delhi, June. Available at http//www.niti.gov.in/writereaddata/files/document_publication/NationalStrategy-for-AI-Discussion-Paper.pdf

Obamuyi, T. and S. Olayiwola. 2019. 'Corruption and Economic Growth in India and Nigeria'. *Journal of Economics and Management*, 35 (1): 80–105.

Ogaki, M., J. Ostry and C. Reinhart. 1996. 'Saving Behavior in Low- and Middle- Income Developing Countries: A Comparison'. IMF Econ Rev., 43, 38–71. Available at: https://doi.org/10.2307/3867352

Olivelle, P. 2011. *Language, Texts, and Society Explorations in Ancient Indian Culture and Religion*, 174. London: Anthem Press.

Ostry, J., P. Loungani and A. Berg. 2018. *Confronting Inequality: How Societies Can Choose Inclusive Growth*. Washington DC: Columbia University Press.

Parida, P. 2009. 'Environmental Awareness in Kautilya's Arthashastra'. Research Paper, Utkal University, Odisha.

Parpola, A. 2007. 'Human Sacrifice in India in Vedic Times and Before', Chapter VIII, in *The Strange World of Human Sacrifice*, edited by J. Bremmer. Leuven, Belgium: Peeters Publishers.

Pathak, P. 2018a. 'Archaeology of Caste System', in *Socio-Economic Dynamics of Indian Society: A Historical Overview*, edited by A. Tilak, D. Jawane, N. Chitnis and R. Vaishampayan. Mumbai: Hindusthan Prakashan Sanstha.

Pathak, P. 2018b. 'Janapadas in Ancient India: Backbone of the Golden Age Economy', in *Socio-Economic Dynamics of Indian Society A Historical Overview*, edited by A. Tilak, D. Jawane, N. Chitnis and R. Vaishampayan. Mumbai: Hindusthan Prakashan Sanstha.

Pillai, R. 2019. *Chanakya Neeti*. Mumbai: Jaico Publishing.

PTI. 2021. 'India Slips Two Spots to Rank 117 on Achieving Sustainable Development Goals: Report'. *The Hindu*, 6 June. Available at: https://www.thehindu.com/news/national/india-slips-two-spots-to-rank-117-on-achieving-sustainable-development-goals-report/article34744187.ece

Rangarajan, L. 1992. *Kautilya: The Arthashastra*. New Delhi: Penguin Books.

Rao, N.. 1970. *The Four Values in Indian Philosophy and Culture*. Mysore: University of Mysore.

Ray, B. 1999. *Tradition and Innovation in Indian Political Thought*. New Delhi: Ajantha Publishers.

Romer, P. 1986. 'Increasing Returns and Long-Run Growth'. *Journal of Political Economy*, 94 (5).

Sanghi, A. 2012. *Chanakya's Chant*. Mumbai: Westland Books.

Sanyal, S. 2013. *Land of the Seven Rivers: A Brief History of India's Geography*. New Delhi: Penguin Random House.

Saran, S. 2018. *How India Sees the World: Kautilya to the 21st Century*. New Delhi: Juggernaut.

Shamasastry, R. 1915. *Kautilya's Arthashastra: Way of Financial Management and Economic Governance*, 177–78). Bottom of the Hill Publishing.

Shamasastry, R. 1917. 'A Note on the Supposed Identity of Vatsayana and Kautilya'. *Quarterly Journal of the Mythic Society*, Vol. 7.

Sihag, B. 2017. 'Kautilya and Machiavelli on Justice, Prosperity and National Security'. *Theoretical Economics Letters*, 7(3): 381–97.

Sihag, B. 2009. 'Kautilya on Administration of Justice during the Fourth Century BC'. *Journal of the History of Economic Thought*, 29 (3): 359–77.

Sihag, B. 2014. *Kautilya: The True Founder of Economics*. New Delhi: Vitasta Publishing.

Singh, S. and A. Sasi. 2018. 'Utilising Idle Gold with Households: Government Schemes Fail to Glitter'. *The Indian Express*, 20 March.

Singh, U. 2008. *A History of Ancient and Early Medieval India: From the Stone Age to the 12th Century*, 261. India: Pearson Education.

Sinha, U.K. 2019. 'Report of the Expert Committee on Micro, Small and Medium Enterprises'. Mumbai: Reserve Bank of India.

Skare, M. 2013. 'The Missing Link from Kautilya's The Arthashastra to Modern Economics'. *The Journal of Philosophical Economics*, May, 6 (2).

Smith, A. 1776. *An Inquiry into the Nature and Causes of the Wealth of Nations*, Book 1, Chapters 1 and 2. New York: Modern Library.

Smith, J. 2020. *The Mahabharata in Sanskrit*. Sacred Texts Archive. Available at: https//www .sacred-texts.com/hin/rys/index.htm (accessed on 3 March 2020).

Solow, R. 1956. 'A Contribution to the Theory of Economic Growth'. *The Quarterly Journal of Economics*, February, 70 (1): 65–94.

Spengler, J. 1971. *Indian Economic Thought*. Durham, North Carolina: Duke University Press.

Spengler, J. 1980. *Origins of Economic Thought and Justice*. Carbondale, Illinois: Southern Illinois University Press.

Srinivasan, T.N. and S.D. Tendulkar. 2003. *Reintegrating India with the World Economy*. Washington DC: Peterson Institute of International Economics.

Sunil, S.S. 1998. 'Contemporaneity of the Perception of the Environment in Kautilya's Arthashastra'. *Indian Journal of History of Science*, 33 (1), 37–50.

Telang, K. 1882. *The Bhagwadgita*. Sacred Text Archive. Available at http//www. sacred-texts.com/hin/sbe08/index.htm

Thiruvadanthai, S. 2018. 'Revisiting India's Growth Experience'. SSRN, 9 August. Available at https://papers.ssrn.com/sol3/papers.cfm?abstract_id=3362842

Trautmann, T. 2012. *Arthashastra: The Science of Wealth*. New Delhi: Allen Lane.

UNICEF. 2017. 'The Financial and Economic Impact of Swacch Bharat Mission in India'. A Report by UNICEF.

UNICEF. 2020. 'Access to Toilets and the Safety, Convenience and Self-Respect of Women in Rural India'. A report by UNICEF.

Verma, R. 2007. 'Savings, Investment and Growth in India: An Application of the ARDL Bounds Testing Approach'. Faculty of Commerce Papers, University of Wollongong, Australia.

Verma Ojha, S. 2016. 'Jambudwipa: The Seeds of Political Unity in the Indian Subcontinent'. *Swarajya*. Available at: https://swarajyamag.com/culture/jambudwipa-the-seeds-of-political-unity-in-the-indian-subcontinent

Verma Ojha, S. 2016. 'Uttarapath and Dakshinapath: The Great Trade Routes of Jambudwipa'. *Swarajya*. Available at: https://swarajyamag.com/culture/uttarapath-and-dakshinapath-the-great-trade-routes-of-jambudwipa

Vinay, V. and M. Hitender. 2017. 'Environment Laws in India', 31 August. Available at https//www.mondaq.com/india/waste-management/624836/environment-laws-in-india

Vinod, H. 2012. 'Preface', in *The Oxford Handbook of Hindu Economics and Business*, edited by H. Vinod. New Delhi: Oxford University Press.

Von Hayek, F. 1974. The Friedrich von Hayek Prize Lecture. Available at https//www.nobelprize.org/prizes/economic-sciences/1974/hayek/lecture/ ().

Waldauer, C., W. Zahka and S. Pal. 1996. 'Kautilya's Arthashastra: A Neglected Precursor to Classical Economics'. *Indian Economic Review*, 31 (1): 101–108.

World Bank. 1992. 'Governance and Development'. International Bank for Reconstruction and Development, Washington DC.

INDEX